THE COMPLETE AIR FRYER COOKBOOK

LINDA LARSEN

THE COMPLETE
AIR FRYER
COOKBOOK

Amazingly Easy Recipes to Fry, Bake, Grill & Roast with Your Air Fryer

FALL RIVER PRESS

New York

FALL RIVER PRESS

New York

An Imprint of Sterling Publishing Co., Inc.
1166 Avenue of the Americas
New York, NY 10036

ISBN 978-1-4351-6607-3

For information about custom editions, special sales, and premium and corporate purchases, please contact Sterling Special Sales at 800-805-5489 or specialsales@sterlingpublishing.com.

Manufactured in China

2 4 6 8 10 9 7 5 3 1

www.sterlingpublishing.com

Photo Credits: Suzanne Clements, cover; Stockfood/Eising Studio – Food Photo & Video, p. 2; Stockfood/PhotoCuisine/Chris Court Photography, p. 8; Stockfood/Valerie Janssen, p. 34; Stocksy/Harald Walker, p. 52; Stockfood/Hein van Tonder,p. 70; Stockfood/Grafe & Unzer Verlag/Thorsten Suedfels, p. 82; Stockfood/Great Stock!, p. 100; Stockfood/ PhotoCuisine/Francoise Nicol, p. 124; Stockfood/Jalag/Julia Hoersch, p. 130

CONTENTS

I dedicate this book to my dear husband Doug, my beautiful nieces Maddie and Grace, and my wonderful nephew Michael. They are a joy and a delight!

INTRODUCTION

The air fryer is a dream machine. That may sound like hyperbole, but it's true. It's hard to resist the taste and texture of fried foods—there's nothing like that crispy mouthfeel when you first bite into a French fry or fried chicken, only to meet the melting and tender interior.

We all know unhealthy fried foods are not meant to be a mainstay in our diet. That's where the air fryer comes in. This appliance produces crisp, moist, and tender foods with little or no oil. With an air fryer, you can eat fried chicken, potato chips, croquettes, doughnuts, egg rolls, shrimp, and tater tots that aren't laden with grease from trans fats. Air-fried foods have the traditional crunch and classic texture of perfectly fried foods, but you can enjoy them guilt-free.

But that's not all the air fryer can make. In addition to fried favorites, you can bake, grill, steam, and roast in your air fryer—and in less time than it takes to cook foods using traditional methods. It's possible to serve risotto, stir-fries, pizzas, casseroles, and desserts from your air fryer in record time, with fabulous results.

When I first used my air fryer, I admit I was hesitant to venture beyond French fries. But when I tossed in some marinated chicken breasts, the result was wonderful; that is, after I learned that marinated foods should be patted dry before cooking! Fortunately, my kitchen fan quickly dispersed the white smoke, and dinner tasted delicious.

In this book, you'll not only learn how to use your air fryer in new and interesting ways but also get acquainted with how the appliance works, discover how to cook prepared frozen foods, find safety tips, and figure out how to solve any problems that may arise with your new dream machine. Let's get frying!

1

FAST FOOD FOR GOOD HEALTH

DEVELOPED IN 2008 IN ENGLAND, a country famous for its fish and chips, the air fryer is a stand-alone appliance that cooks, bakes, fries, grills, and steams food to tender perfection. This heavy-duty appliance was embraced soon after in the United States for its quick cooking ability and versatility.

The air fryer consists of a heating element, a frying basket attached to a pan that catches the juices and fat released as the food cooks, and a fan that pushes hot air around the food. The heating element browns and crisps the exterior while cooking the interior to a safe final temperature.

There are two kinds of cooking methods: dry heat, such as frying; and wet heat, such as steaming or braising. Surprisingly, cooking food in oil is considered a dry-heat cooking method. The air fryer takes this method one step further by eliminating the oil altogether.

FIVE BENEFITS OF AIR FRYING

Still wondering if you made the right decision when you purchased an air fryer? Wonder no more.

Air frying is better for your health. In fact, most recipes cook without any added fat. The recipes that do use oil use only a very small amount for flavor, usually just a few teaspoons. If there is too much oil on the food, it will melt off, and the appliance may emit smoke.

It's very safe, even for beginning cooks. The system is completely closed, unlike deep-frying in a pan on the stovetop. There's no danger of a pan full of hot oil falling off the stove. Because the machine is closed while it's cooking, you won't burn your fingers or be splattered with hot liquid as the food cooks.

Most air fryers have automatic cooking functions, so there's no guess-work. Depending on the model you choose, you can cook French fries, chicken fingers, tater tots, and other foods with just a press of a button. The machine controls the cooking times and cooking temperatures of these foods for you.

Cleanup is a breeze. Air fryers are made with nonstick material, so, to clean, you simply wash the basket and pan in the sink with soap and water, using a sponge that won't scratch. If any food is burned onto the basket, a quick soak will loosen it. The appliance itself can be cleaned with a damp paper towel or sponge. You don't have to worry about safely disposing of cups of oil.

Using only one appliance to prepare your food is extremely convenient. The cooking method is hands-free, so you can prepare a salad while your food cooks. If you have a small kitchen, this may be the only appliance you need.

STEP-BY-STEP AIR FRYING

An air fryer is basically a miniature convection oven: A fan blows heated air over food to cook it quickly. Here are the keys to using it well.

1. **If your air fryer is new, clean it.** Remove the basket and pan along with any accessories, and wash them with soap and water. Use a damp paper towel to clean the outside and inside of the air fryer. Dry off all of the components, and familiarize yourself with the instructions.

2. **Prepare your food.** Cut food into similar-size pieces so they cook evenly. If you want to marinate food, plan ahead. (Most foods only need to marinate for a few minutes, but for really deep flavor, you may want to marinate overnight in the refrigerator.) Then, pat the pieces dry. Any excess liquid on foods will drip into the pan and may cause the appliance to smoke.

3. **If needed, preheat.** Some air fryer models require preheating; others do not. Read the instruction manual for your appliance.

4. **If you are going to coat food with crumbs,** make sure that the coating is patted firmly onto the food. Spray other foods lightly with cooking spray or oil from a mister. Then, put the food into the basket or baking pan.

5. **If you are going to use a pan,** use the size recommended by the instruction manual. Most air fryers use a 6-by-6-by-2-inch pan, and the recipes in this book were developed for that size. Spray the pan with nonstick cooking spray, or line it with parchment paper liners that come with tabs to easily remove food. You can also use a 6-inch metal bowl as long it fits easily in the basket with room to spare on the top. The metal will be very hot, so to remove the pan or bowl, use spring-loaded tongs.

THE MAILLARD REACTION

This phrase is the name for the chemical reaction between an amino acid and a sugar that occurs on the surface of foods when cooked at high heat. The technical term is "nonenzymatic browning," which just means the reaction occurs without enzymes. (When apples and avocados are cut, this is caused by enzymatic browning.) The Maillard reaction gives food its characteristic brown color and produces the hundreds of flavor and aroma compounds that make fried foods taste and smell so good. Heat increases the rate of this reaction.

In order for foods to brown in the Maillard reaction, they need protein, sugar, heat, and surface dryness. Moist or wet foods will not brown well, which is another reason it's important to dry foods before they are cooked in an air fryer. Adding a tiny bit of sugar or a pinch of baking soda to foods can increase browning.

6. **Place the basket into the air fryer and set the time.** Don't overcrowd food in the basket. If you're cooking small items, such as tater tots or chopped vegetables, shake the food halfway through the cooking time. Remove the basket with the pan attached, and shake gently to redistribute the food. Some recipes ask you to turn food. **Never** use your fingers; use tongs or a large fork for this step.

7. **When the food is done, remove the basket,** with the pan in it, if used, and take the food out with tongs. Never tip the basket with the pan attached into a dish; any liquids or grease in the pan will spill onto the food and may burn your fingers.

AIR FRYER COOKING CHART

Your air fryer may have its own cooking times and temperatures; always follow the instructions that came with your appliance. And always cook foods, especially meats, poultry, and seafood, until done to a safe internal temperature. But you can use this general chart for reference.

VEGETABLES			
French fries (thin, frozen)	2 to 4 cups	390°F	10 to 14 minutes
If you find ice on the fries, remove it; toss once during cooking.			
French fries (thin, fresh)	2 to 4 cups	400°F	15 to 20 minutes
Pat dry; toss with cornstarch and ½ teaspoon sugar for better browning, then mist with oil; toss once during cooking.			
French fries (thick, frozen)	2 to 4 cups	380°F	12 to 20 minutes
If you find ice on the fries, remove it.			
French fries (thick, fresh)	2 to 4 cups	400°F	15 to 25 minutes
Lightly spray with oil.			
Potato wedges	2 to 4 cups	390°F	18 to 22 minutes
Lightly spray with oil; sprinkle with salt and pepper.			

Chips	3 to 7 cups	400°F	7 to 12 minutes

Toss once or twice during cooking.

Chopped potatoes	4 to 7 cups	400°F	13 to 19 minutes

Spray with oil; toss once or twice during cooking.

Potato slices	4 to 5 cups	380°F	10 to 15 minutes

Slice about ⅛-inch thick; spray with oil; toss during cooking.

Cauliflower florets	2 to 4 cups	390°F	5 to 9 minutes

Mist with oil and season before frying; toss once during cooking.

Other Vegetables	1 to 3 pounds	350°F	Sliced eggplant: 15 to 20 minutes Zucchini: 10 minutes Onions: 4 to 7 minutes Tomatoes: Whole for 8 minutes, Slices for 4 minutes Green beans: Whole for 5 to 7 minutes

Cook vegetables individually; sliced onions work better than chopped; cut to similar sizes; toss once during cooking.

POULTRY AND MEAT			
Chicken nuggets	1 to 4 cups	370°F	7 to 12 minutes
If you find ice on the chicken, remove it.			
Chicken wings	1 to 3 pounds	380°F	15 to 20 minutes
Cook to an internal temperature of 165°F; toss once during cooking.			
Chicken drumsticks	1 to 6 drumsticks	400°F and 320°F	8 minutes at 400°F, then 10 to 12 minutes at 320°F
Pat dry; do not rinse. Spray with oil and sprinkle with seasonings.			
Chicken breast	1 to 6 6-ounce boneless, skinless halves	360°F	10 to 16 minutes
Place in a single layer in the basket; turn once during cooking.			
Pork chops	1 to 4 1-inch thick chops	350°F	7 to 10 minutes
Cook to a minimum internal temperature of 145°F. Place in a single layer; turn once during cooking (optional).			
Burgers	1 to 4 4-ounce patties	360°F	6 to 9 minutes
Place in single layer; turn once during cooking. Cook to a minimum internal temperature of 160°F.			
Frozen meatballs	25 per batch	380°F	6 to 8 minutes
If you find ice on the meatballs, remove it.			

Raw meatballs	25 per batch	390°F	6 to 9 minutes

Don't crowd; place in a single layer in the basket; turn with tongs halfway through cooking time.

Steak	1 to 4 6-ounce steaks, ¾ inch thick	360°F	8 to 12 minutes

Time depends on desired doneness; use a food thermometer to cook to 140°F for medium rare; 160°F for well done.

FISH			
Fish sticks (frozen)	1 to 3 cups	390°F	8 to 10 minutes

If you find ice on the fish, remove it.

Shrimp (frozen)	1 to 2 pounds	390°F	8 minutes

If you find ice on the shrimp, remove it; can bread before cooking.

Shrimp (fresh)	1 to 2 pounds	390°F	5 minutes

Shell and devein shrimp; pat dry. Can bread before cooking.

Salmon fillets	4 6-ounce fillets	300°F	9 to 14 minutes

Brush with oil and sprinkle with seasonings before cooking to an internal temperature of 140°F.

Salmon steak	4 8-ounce steaks	300°F	14 to 18 minutes

Brush with oil and sprinkle with seasonings; cook to an internal temperature of 140°F.

OTHER			
Egg rolls	6 to 8	390°F	3 to 6 minutes
Brush or mist with oil before cooking.			
Pizza	1 pizza	390°F	5 to 10 minutes
Place pizza on parchment paper in the basket. Make sure it fits into the basket.			
Grilled cheese sandwiches	1 to 3 sandwiches	400°F	7 minutes
Place on parchment paper; turn with tongs halfway through cooking.			
Cake	1 8-inch pan	320°F	20 to 25 minutes
Use a cake pan that fits easily inside the basket.			
Muffins	10 muffins	360°F	10 to 12 minutes
Muffins should be placed inside double foil cups; place in single layer.			
Fruit	2 to 4 cups	320°F	3 to 5 minutes for soft fruits; 5 to 10 minutes for hard fruits
Cook hard fruits, such as apples, and soft fruits, such as peaches, separately.			

STRAIGHT FROM THE STORE

For the ultimate in quick cooking and convenience, some foods can be dropped into the air fryer as is. You can cook frozen French fries (curly fried or straight), tater tots, bread dough, puff pastry, vegetables (such as cauliflower florets, bell pepper strips, and carrot sticks), baby potatoes, frozen waffles and pancakes, and whole nuts in the air fryer, just as they come out of the bag or box. Meats and fish that you can drop into the air fryer include frozen chicken nuggets, chicken drumsticks, and chicken wings, fish sticks, fish fillets, salmon fillets and steaks, beef steaks, and pre-marinated meats (after patting them dry).

In fact, many air fryers have automatic cooking times set into the appliance for each food, so you don't have to guess about the time or temperature. Read through the instruction manual for the foods that can be cooked with the single push of a button.

HEALTHY OILS

While the air fryer doesn't need oil to turn out beautifully bronzed, crisp food, some recipes call for the addition of a small amount of oil. The best oils to use have a "high smoke point," that is, the temperature at which they begin to smoke. Those oils are refined peanut oil, refined safflower oil, refined grapeseed oil, refined corn oil, and extra light olive oil (not to be confused with extra virgin olive oil, which has a lower smoke point).

The healthiest fat for cooking is olive oil. This oil can raise the good cholesterol and reduce bad cholesterol in your blood because it contains monounsaturated fatty acids (MUFAs). Using olive oil in cooking may also reduce the risk of developing type 2 diabetes, lower cholesterol levels, and reduce the risk of a stroke.

If you don't like using artificial cooking sprays, buy an oil mister and add the oil of your choice. This is the best way to evenly coat foods with a little bit of oil.

AIR FRYER SAFETY

As safe as this appliance is, you still need to handle it with care. Read through the instruction manual for basic safety tips.

Always place the air fryer on a stable, even, and heat-proof surface. I like to put mine on my smooth ceramic cooktop (turned off, of course).

While the fryer is cooking, steam will be released from the vents. This steam can be hot, so stay away from the appliance, and keep your hands and face away from the vents.

When you remove the basket from the air fryer, don't touch the basket or the pan it's attached to because they will be very hot. Never tip food out of the fryer. The pan may have hot oil or liquid in it, and tipping it will spill that liquid over the food and it may splash on you. And never press the button holding the basket and pan together when you remove them; that could cause burns.

Always cook ground beef and pork to 160°F, ground turkey and chicken to 165°F, pork to 145°F, chicken to 165°F, and fish to 140°F for food safety reasons. Use a food thermometer to make sure these meats are cooked to the correct temperature.

PROBLEM SOLVING

Again, because all air fryers are a bit different, you'll want to read the manual that comes with your appliance. Each machine may have different cooking times and temperatures for different foods.

I have found that shaking the basket when cooking small items and turning larger pieces, such as sandwiches and pork chops, gives food an appetizing color and crisp texture. Adding a bit of oil using your mister or a brush also makes food taste deep-fried.

If the food isn't crisp, it may have been too wet when you placed it in the fryer. Before cooking, pat dry such foods as marinated chicken and vegetables. Smoke coming from the machine is another problem. White smoke means that foods are too wet or have a lot of fat; some of that smoke may

PAIRING RECIPES

Some air fryers come with a separator panel that you can use to cook two different kinds of food at the same time. Look in the instruction manual or in this book and find foods that cook at the same temperature. The timing doesn't have to be exactly the same, since you can remove the food that is cooked and return the basket to the fryer to finish cooking the other food.

Some examples include steak with vegetables, chicken breasts with potato wedges, and fish sticks with thick French fries (or chips, as the Brits call them). If the cooking temperature is close (say, one cooks at 350°F and another at 360°F), you can adjust the cooking time slightly to accommodate the difference.

Practice makes perfect, so don't hesitate to experiment. Just make sure that you cook meats, seafood, and poultry to safe internal temperatures.

just be steam, or the result of particles of food that were stuck to the inside of the fryer. Black smoke, however, is a sign of a real problem and may mean the machine is malfunctioning. If this happens, turn it off, unplug it, let it cool, and take it to a repair shop or contact the manufacturer.

CLEANING AND CARING FOR YOUR AIR FRYER

The instruction manual will have specifics about how to clean and care for your machine. Remember that the air fryer is not a toy, but cooking equipment, and should be treated with care.

Let the machine cool down before attempting to clean. Remove the basket and pan and wash with soap and water and a plastic scrubbing brush. If food is stuck on these pieces, let them soak in warm water for 10 to 20 minutes, then clean. Some parts may be dishwasher-safe; check the instruction manual.

Make sure that you always check inside the appliance for stray crumbs or bits of food and remove them. Wipe the appliance—turned off, unplugged, and cooled down—both inside and outside with a damp towel, sponge, or paper towel. If grease or oil has fallen to the bottom of the pan, soak it up with paper towels, then wipe clean.

ABOUT THE RECIPES

The recipes in this book were chosen for appeal, ease of preparation, and speed. Each recipe is labeled with a few defining words:

- Fast
- Family Favorite
- Vegetarian
- Vegan
- Gluten-Free

Fast recipes will be ready to eat in 15 minutes or less, start to finish. Family Favorite recipes serve at least four people and use kid-friendly ingredients.

Some of these recipes reproduce deep-fried foods, while others are cooked with steam (with a little liquid in the pan holding the basket), while others are baked, grilled, or stir-fried. When you first make these recipes, use the shortest cooking time, because every air fryer is different. If you need to add more time, you can, but you can't undo overcooked or burned food.

Once you get the hang of your air fryer, you can branch out and even experiment a little. Try making chips using other vegetables that are thinly sliced and patted dry. Try using other herbs and spices in place of the ones called for in the recipe, or substitute different vegetables or fruits. Most of all, enjoy!

2

BREAKFAST

Shrimp and Rice Frittata

PREP TIME: 15 MINUTES / COOK TIME: 15 MINUTES / SERVES 4

**320°F
BAKE**

GLUTEN-FREE

4 eggs

Pinch salt

½ teaspoon
dried basil

Nonstick
cooking spray

½ cup cooked
rice

½ cup chopped
cooked
shrimp

½ cup baby
spinach

½ cup grated
Monterey Jack
or Cojack
cheese

Make this recipe even easier by using leftover rice or rice from your favorite Asian restaurant. You can also buy frozen rice that's easily thawed by running hot water over the package.

1. In a small bowl, beat the eggs with the salt and basil until frothy. Spray a 6-by-6-by-2-inch pan with nonstick cooking spray.
2. Combine the rice, shrimp, and spinach in the prepared pan. Pour the eggs in and sprinkle with the cheese.
3. Bake for 14 to 18 minutes or until the frittata is puffed and golden brown.

....

Substitution tip: *This recipe can be changed to suit your taste. If you don't like shrimp, use cooked sausages or chopped cooked chicken. Or omit the spinach and use chopped bell peppers or frozen baby peas instead.*

....

Per serving: Calories: 226; Total Fat: 9g; Saturated Fat: 4g; Cholesterol: 221mg; Sodium: 232mg; Carbohydrates: 19; Fiber: 0g; Protein: 16g

Scotch Eggs

PREP TIME: 15 MINUTES / COOK TIME: 12 MINUTES / SERVES 6

Scotch eggs are an English classic made with a hard-cooked egg encased in pork sausage and deep-fried. Here you'll lighten up the recipe by using chicken sausage and cooking it in the air fryer. Serve with a fruit salad and some cinnamon rolls or muffins for a celebratory breakfast.

1. Peel the hard-cooked eggs and set aside.
2. In a large bowl, combine the chicken sausage, one raw egg, and ½ cup of the bread crumbs, and mix well. Divide into six pieces and flatten each into a long oval.
3. In a shallow bowl, beat the remaining two raw eggs.
4. Roll each hard-cooked egg in the flour and wrap one of the chicken sausage pieces around the egg to completely encircle it.
5. Roll the egg first in the flour, then dip in the beaten eggs, and finally dip in the remaining bread crumbs to coat. Prepare the remaining eggs the same way.
6. Place the eggs in a single layer in the air fryer and spray with oil.
7. Air-fry for 6 minutes, then turn using tongs and mist with more oil. Air-fry for 5 to 7 minutes or until the chicken is thoroughly cooked and the Scotch eggs are brown.

....

Did You Know? *You can buy hard-cooked eggs, already peeled, at many grocery stores! Look for them in the dairy case, and make sure to follow expiration dates to the letter. Or hard-cook them right in your air fryer (Hard-Cooked Eggs, page 24).*

....

Per serving: Calories: 623; Total Fat: 40g; Saturated Fat: 13g; Cholesterol: 341mg; Sodium: 1,140mg; Carbohydrates: 28g; Fiber: 2g; Protein: 35g

370°F FRY

FAMILY FAVORITE

6 hard-cooked eggs
1½ pounds bulk lean chicken or turkey sausage
3 raw eggs, divided
1½ cups dried bread crumbs, divided
½ cup flour
Oil, for misting

Omelette in Bread Cups

PREP TIME: 12 MINUTES / COOK TIME: 11 MINUTES / SERVES 4

**330°F
BAKE**

FAMILY FAVORITE

4 (3-by-4-inch)
    crusty rolls
4 thin slices
    Gouda or
    Swiss cheese
    mini wedges
5 eggs
2 tablespoons
    heavy cream
½ teaspoon
    dried thyme
3 strips
    precooked
    bacon,
    chopped
Pinch salt
Freshly ground
    black pepper

Serving an omelette in a bread cup is a fun twist on a breakfast classic. The bread becomes crisp and toasted, while the eggs stay moist and fluffy. You can substitute different ingredients to add to the eggs, but bacon and cheese make a perfect savory combo.

1. Cut the tops off the rolls and remove the insides with your fingers to make a shell with about ½ inch of bread remaining. Line the rolls with a slice of cheese, pressing down gently so the cheese conforms to the inside of the roll.
2. In a medium bowl, beat the eggs with the heavy cream until combined. Stir in the thyme, bacon, and salt and pepper.
3. Spoon the egg mixture into the rolls over the cheese.
4. Bake for 8 to 12 minutes or until the eggs are puffy and starting to brown on top.

....

Ingredient tip: *Freeze the leftover bread for a later use as homemade bread crumbs. They are much tastier than store-bought bread crumbs.*

....

Per serving: Calories: 499; Total Fat: 24g; Saturated Fat: 9g; Cholesterol: 250mg; Sodium: 1,025mg; Carbohydrates: 46g; Fiber: 2g; Protein: 25g

Mixed Berry Muffins

PREP TIME: 15 MINUTES / COOK TIME: 30 MINUTES / MAKES 8 MUFFINS

This easy recipe makes eight light and tender muffins that your entire family will love. Choose your favorite fresh berries: chopped strawberries, blueberries, and raspberries are all delicious.

**320°F
BAKE**

**FAMILY FAVORITE,
VEGETARIAN**

1. In medium bowl, combine the 1⅓ cups flour, baking powder, white sugar, and brown sugar, and mix well.
2. In small bowl, combine the eggs, milk, and oil, and beat until combined. Stir the egg mixture into the dry ingredients just until combined.
3. In another small bowl, toss the mixed berries with the remaining 1 tablespoon of flour until coated. Stir gently into the batter.
4. Double up 16 foil muffin cups to make 8 cups. Put 4 cups into the air fryer and fill three-quarters full with the batter. Bake for 12 to 17 minutes or until the tops of the muffins spring back when lightly touched with your finger.
5. Repeat with the remaining muffin cups and batter. Cool on a wire rack for 10 minutes before serving.

1⅓ cups plus
  1 tablespoon
  flour
2 teaspoons
  baking
  powder
¼ cup white
  sugar
2 tablespoons
  brown sugar
2 eggs
⅔ cup whole
  milk
⅓ cup safflower
  oil
1 cup mixed
  fresh berries

....

Did You Know? *You can use frozen berries in this recipe, but don't thaw them before use. If frozen berries are thawed they will make the batter too wet, and the berries may stain the batter.*

....

Per serving: Calories: 230; Total Fat: 11g; Saturated Fat: 2g; Cholesterol: 43mg; Sodium: 26mg; Carbohydrates: 30g; Fiber: 1g; Protein: 4g

Cranberry Beignets

PREP TIME: 15 MINUTES / COOK TIME: 8 MINUTES / MAKES 16 BEIGNETS

330°F
FRY

FAMILY FAVORITE,
VEGETARIAN

1½ cups flour

2 teaspoons
baking soda

¼ teaspoon salt

3 tablespoons
brown sugar

⅓ cup chopped
dried
cranberries

½ cup buttermilk

1 egg

3 tablespoons
melted
unsalted
butter

Beignets were made famous at New Orleans' Café du Monde, which serves the little puffs with hot, freshly brewed chicory coffee. These beignets have chopped dried cranberries stirred into the dough, which adds wonderful flavor and color. This is a baking powder beignet recipe, which means you don't have to wait for a yeast dough to rise.

1. In a medium bowl, combine the flour, baking soda, salt, and brown sugar, and mix well. Stir in dried cranberries.
2. In a small bowl, combine the buttermilk and egg, and beat until smooth. Stir into the dry ingredients just until moistened.
3. Pat the dough into an 8-by-8-inch square and cut into 16 pieces. Coat each piece lightly with melted butter.
4. Place in a single layer in the air fryer basket, making sure the pieces don't touch. You may have to cook in batches depending on the size of your air fryer basket. Air-fry for 5 to 8 minutes or until puffy and golden brown. Dust with powdered sugar before serving, if desired.

....

Did You Know? *Using unsalted butter ensures food will not stick to the air fryer basket when cooking. Salt in butter can make foods stick, which is not what you want.*

....

Per serving: Calories: 76; Total Fat: 3g; Saturated Fat: 2g; Cholesterol: 16mg; Sodium: 221mg; Carbohydrates: 11g; Fiber: 0g; Protein: 2g

Dutch Pancake

PREP TIME: 12 MINUTES / COOK TIME: 15 MINUTES / SERVES 4

A Dutch pancake is made from a batter cooked quickly at high heat so it puffs up in the oven. When you take it out of the oven, it falls, making a natural well to fill with just about anything—from scrambled eggs to fresh fruits to lots of syrup. Enjoy with turkey bacon and a cold glass of orange juice.

1. Preheat the air fryer with a 6-by-6-by-2-inch pan in the basket. Add the butter and heat until the butter melts.
2. Meanwhile, in a medium bowl, add the eggs, flour, milk, and vanilla, and beat well with an eggbeater until combined and frothy.
3. Carefully remove the basket with the pan from the air fryer and tilt so the butter covers the bottom of the pan. Immediately pour in the batter and put back in the fryer.
4. Bake for 12 to 16 minutes or until the pancake is puffed and golden brown.
5. Remove from the oven; the pancake will fall. Top with strawberries and powdered sugar and serve immediately.

....

Substitution tip: *This pancake can be served with savory fillings, too. Add some crisply cooked bacon, hot cooked sausage, or cheese that will melt on the crisp and hot pancake.*

....

Per serving: Calories: 196; Total Fat: 9g; Saturated Fat: 5g; Cholesterol: 138mg; Sodium: 96mg; Carbohydrates: 22g; Fiber: 2g; Protein: 7g

330°F BAKE

FAMILY FAVORITE, VEGETARIAN

2 (scant) tablespoons unsalted butter

3 eggs

½ cup flour

½ cup milk

½ teaspoon vanilla

1½ cups sliced fresh strawberries

2 tablespoons powdered sugar

Monkey Bread

PREP TIME: 7 MINUTES / COOK TIME: 8 MINUTES / SERVES 4

350°F BAKE

FAST, FAMILY FAVORITE, VEGETARIAN

1 (8-ounce) can refrigerated biscuits

¼ cup white sugar

3 tablespoons brown sugar

½ teaspoon cinnamon

⅛ teaspoon nutmeg

3 tablespoons melted unsalted butter

Monkey bread may be a strange name for a breakfast pastry that contains no bananas! Instead, biscuit dough is cut into pieces, coated in butter, sugar, and spices, and baked. When it's done baking, simply pull off pieces of the sweet bread and enjoy warm.

1. Open the can of biscuits, separate, and cut each biscuit into 4 pieces.
2. Combine the white sugar, brown sugar, cinnamon, and nutmeg in a shallow bowl and mix well.
3. Dip each biscuit briefly into the butter and roll in the sugar mixture to coat. Place in a 6-by-6-by-2-inch baking pan.
4. Bake for 6 to 9 minutes or until golden brown. Let cool for 5 minutes, then serve. Be careful when eating at first, because the sugar gets very hot.

....

Did You Know? *The origin of the Monkey Bread name is lost in the annals of history. Some people think it got its name because it looks like the Monkey Puzzle tree. Or it may be that the bread is "as much fun as a barrel of monkeys."*

....

Per serving: Calories: 393; Total Fat: 17g; Saturated Fat: 8g; Cholesterol: 24mg; Sodium: 787mg; Carbohydrates: 55g; Fiber: 1g; Protein: 5g

Chocolate-Filled Doughnut Holes

PREP TIME: 10 MINUTES / COOK TIME: 12 MINUTES /
MAKES 24 DOUGHNUT HOLES

Doughnut holes are the little round puffs that are removed when doughnuts are formed. In this case, you use biscuit dough and wrap each piece around a chocolate chip. When baked, the chocolate inside melts, making a decadent breakfast treat.

1. Separate and cut each biscuit into thirds.
2. Flatten each biscuit piece slightly and put 1 to 2 chocolate chips in the center. Wrap the dough around the chocolate and seal the edges well.
3. Brush each doughnut hole with a bit of the butter and air-fry in batches for 8 to 12 minutes.
4. Remove and dust with powdered sugar. Serve warm.

....

Variation tip: *Get creative with the fillings for these little doughnut holes. Use a combination of chocolate chips and nuts, or try chopped-up candy bars. Just make sure the dough isn't filled too tightly, or the holes may split during air frying.*

....

Per serving: Calories: 393; Total Fat: 17g; Saturated Fat: 8g; Cholesterol: 24mg; Sodium: 787mg; Carbohydrates: 55g; Fiber: 1g; Protein: 5g

340°F FRY

FAMILY FAVORITE, VEGETARIAN

1 (8-count) can refrigerated biscuits

24 to 48 semisweet chocolate chips

3 tablespoons melted unsalted butter

¼ cup powdered sugar

3

LUNCH

Vegetable Egg Rolls

PREP TIME: 15 MINUTES / COOK TIME: 10 MINUTES / MAKES 8 EGG ROLLS

**390°F
FRY**

**FAMILY FAVORITE,
VEGETARIAN**

½ cup chopped
    mushrooms
½ cup grated
    carrots
½ cup chopped
    zucchini
2 green onions,
    chopped
2 tablespoons
    low-sodium
    soy sauce
8 egg roll
    wrappers
1 tablespoon
    cornstarch
1 egg, beaten

Egg rolls and the air fryer are a perfect match. The wrapping gets so crisp and light, and the filling is perfectly heated—all with very little oil! Enjoy these for lunch with soy or sweet-and-sour dipping sauces.

1. In a medium bowl, combine the mushrooms, carrots, zucchini, green onions, and soy sauce, and stir together.
2. Place the egg roll wrappers on a work surface. Top each with about 3 tablespoons of the vegetable mixture.
3. In a small bowl, combine the cornstarch and egg and mix well. Brush some of this mixture on the edges of the egg roll wrappers. Roll up the wrappers, enclosing the vegetable filling. Brush some of the egg mixture on the outside of the egg rolls to seal.
4. Air-fry for 7 to 10 minutes or until the egg rolls are brown and crunchy.

....

Substitution tip: *You can use spring roll wrappers for this recipe; they are thinner than the egg roll wrappers so they won't take as long to cook.*

....

Calories: 112; Total Fat: 1g; Saturated Fat: 0g; Cholesterol: 23mg; Sodium: 417mg; Carbohydrates: 21g; Fiber: 1g; Protein: 4g

Veggies on Toast

PREP TIME: 12 MINUTES / COOK TIME: 11 MINUTES / SERVES 4

In this easy, healthy recipe, roasted vegetables top toasted bread that is spread with soft goat cheese. You can use any tender veggies you'd like. Root vegetables, such as potatoes or carrots, will take longer to roast and shouldn't be combined with the softer produce.

**330°F
ROAST**

VEGETARIAN

1 red bell pepper, cut into ½-inch strips

1 cup sliced button or cremini mushrooms

1 small yellow squash, sliced

2 green onions, cut into ½-inch slices

Extra light olive oil for misting

4 to 6 pieces sliced French or Italian bread

2 tablespoons softened butter

½ cup soft goat cheese

1. Combine the red pepper, mushrooms, squash, and green onions in the air fryer and mist with oil. Roast for 7 to 9 minutes or until the vegetables are tender, shaking the basket once during cooking time.
2. Remove the vegetables from the basket and set aside.
3. Spread the bread with butter and place in the air fryer, butter-side up. Toast for 2 to 4 minutes or until golden brown.
4. Spread the goat cheese on the toasted bread and top with the vegetables; serve warm.

....

Variation tip: *To add even more flavor, drizzle the finished toasts with extra-virgin olive oil and balsamic vinegar.*

....

Calories: 162; Total Fat: 11g; Saturated Fat: 7g; Cholesterol: 30mg; Sodium: 160mg; Carbohydrates: 9g; Fiber: 2g; Protein: 7g

Jumbo Stuffed Mushrooms

PREP TIME: 10 MINUTES / COOK TIME: 8 MINUTES / SERVES 4

**390°F
BAKE**

VEGETARIAN

4 jumbo
   portobello
   mushrooms
1 tablespoon
   olive oil
¼ cup ricotta
   cheese
5 tablespoons
   Parmesan
   cheese,
   divided
1 cup frozen
   chopped
   spinach,
   thawed and
   drained
⅓ cup bread
   crumbs
¼ teaspoon
   minced fresh
   rosemary

If you look in the produce section, you can often find portobello mushrooms that are about 3 inches in diameter. These mushrooms are large enough—and satisfying enough—that one makes a lunch-size serving. The cheesy spinach filling is made fragrant with fresh rosemary.

1. Wipe the mushrooms with a damp cloth. Remove the stems and discard. Using a spoon, gently scrape out most of the gills.
2. Rub the mushrooms with the olive oil. Put in the air fryer basket, hollow side up, and bake for 3 minutes. Carefully remove the mushroom caps, because they will contain liquid. Drain the liquid out of the caps.
3. In a medium bowl, combine the ricotta, 3 tablespoons of Parmesan cheese, spinach, bread crumbs, and rosemary, and mix well.
4. Stuff this mixture into the drained mushroom caps. Sprinkle with the remaining 2 tablespoons of Parmesan cheese. Put the mushroom caps back into the basket.
5. Bake for 4 to 6 minutes or until the filling is hot and the mushroom caps are tender.

....

Did You Know? *The gills in large mushroom caps are edible, but they can be bitter when cooked. You can easily remove them with a spoon.*

....

Per serving: Calories: 117; Total Fat: 7g; Saturated Fat: 3g; Cholesterol: 10mg; Sodium: 180mg; Carbohydrates: 8g; Fiber: 1g; Protein: 7g

Mushroom Pita Pizzas

PREP TIME: 10 MINUTES / COOK TIME: 5 MINUTES / SERVES 4

Pita bread makes a great crust for a super-quick pizza. The bread becomes crisp and crunchy, while the cheese gets all bubbly and brown in the air fryer. You can use this basic method to make pizza with just about any cooked topping, such as meat or veggies.

360°F BAKE

FAST, VEGETARIAN

4 (3-inch) pitas
1 tablespoon olive oil
¾ cup pizza sauce
1 (4-ounce) jar sliced mushrooms, drained
½ teaspoon dried basil
2 green onions, minced
1 cup grated mozzarella or provolone cheese
1 cup sliced grape tomatoes

1. Brush each piece of pita with oil and top with the pizza sauce.
2. Add the mushrooms and sprinkle with basil and green onions. Top with the grated cheese.
3. Bake for 3 to 6 minutes or until the cheese is melted and starts to brown. Top with the grape tomatoes and serve immediately.

....

Substitution tip: *Look for canned pizza sauce in the pasta aisle of the supermarket. Or, substitute ¾ cup pasta sauce mixed with a pinch each of dried basil, thyme, oregano, marjoram, and cayenne pepper.*

....

Per serving: Calories: 231; Total Fat: 9g; Saturated Fat: 4g; Cholesterol: 15mg; Sodium: 500mg; Carbohydrates: 25g; Fiber: 2g; Protein: 13g

Spinach Quiche

PREP TIME: 10 MINUTES / COOK TIME: 20 MINUTES / SERVES 3

320°F BAKE

VEGETARIAN, GLUTEN-FREE

3 eggs

1 cup frozen chopped spinach, thawed and drained

⅓ cup heavy cream

2 tablespoons honey mustard

½ cup grated Swiss or Havarti cheese

½ teaspoon dried thyme

Pinch salt

Freshly ground black pepper

Nonstick baking spray with flour

A crustless quiche is not only quick to pull together, it's less dense than the original. This recipe satisfies for a no-fuss lunch and tastes even better the next day, eaten cold.

1. In a medium bowl, beat the eggs until blended. Stir in the spinach, cream, honey mustard, cheese, thyme, salt, and pepper.
2. Spray a 6-by-6-by-2-inch pan baking pan with nonstick spray. Pour the egg mixture into the pan.
3. Bake for 18 to 22 minutes or until the egg mixture is puffed, light golden brown, and set.
4. Let cool for 5 minutes, then cut into wedges to serve.

....

Substitution tip: *You could use just about any cooked, leftover vegetable in this easy recipe as long as you keep the amounts about the same. Try adding cooked broccoli florets, steamed asparagus pieces, or cooked mushrooms.*

....

Per serving: Calories: 203; Total Fat: 15g; Saturated Fat: 8g; Cholesterol: 199mg; Sodium: 211mg; Carbohydrates: 6g; Fiber: 0g; Protein: 11g

Yellow Squash Fritters

PREP TIME: 15 MINUTES / COOK TIME: 8 MINUTES / SERVES 4

Fritters are usually made with shredded vegetables mixed with cheese and egg, and fried in fat until they are browned and crisp. The air fryer makes them with very little fat, but they still retain the crunchy exterior and delicious, dense interior.

1. In a medium bowl, combine the cream cheese, egg, oregano, and salt and pepper. Add the squash and carrot, and mix well. Stir in the bread crumbs.
2. Form about 2 tablespoons of this mixture into a patty about ½ inch thick. Repeat with remaining mixture. Brush the fritters with olive oil.
3. Air-fry until crisp and golden, about 7 to 9 minutes.

....

Cooking tip: *Yellow summer squash has a thin skin so you don't have to peel it before preparation. If you want to use zucchini in this recipe, peel it before grating, because the skin is tougher.*

....

Per serving: Calories: 234; Total Fat: 17g; Saturated Fat: 6g; Cholesterol: 64mg; Sodium: 261mg; Carbohydrates: 16g; Fiber: 2g; Protein: 6g

340°F FRY

FAMILY FAVORITE, VEGETARIAN

1 (3-ounce) package cream cheese, softened
1 egg, beaten
½ teaspoon dried oregano
Pinch salt
Freshly ground black pepper
1 medium yellow summer squash, grated
⅓ cup grated carrot
⅔ cup bread crumbs
2 tablespoons olive oil

Pesto Gnocchi

PREP TIME: 5 MINUTES / COOK TIME: 20 MINUTES / SERVES 4

**390°F
BAKE**

VEGETARIAN

1 tablespoon
olive oil

1 onion, finely
chopped

3 cloves garlic,
sliced

1 (16-ounce)
package shelf-
stable gnocchi

1 (8-ounce) jar
pesto

⅓ cup grated
Parmesan
cheese

Gnocchi can be found in the pasta section of the supermarket, in a shelf-stable package that doesn't need refrigeration. When cooked in the air fryer, the result is different than when you boil them; expect a crisp and tender bite.

1. Combine the oil, onion, garlic, and gnocchi in a 6-by-6-by-2-inch pan and put into the air fryer.
2. Bake for 10 minutes, then remove the pan and stir.
3. Return the pan to the air fryer and cook for 8 to 13 minutes or until the gnocchi are lightly browned and crisp.
4. Remove the pan from the air fryer. Stir in the pesto and Parmesan cheese, and serve immediately.

....

Did You Know? *Gnocchi is pronounced "nyuk-ee." They are little oval dumplings about 1 inch long with ridges on one side. They can be fried, baked, or boiled.*

....

Per serving: Calories: 646; Total Fat: 32g; Saturated Fat: 7g; Cholesterol: 103mg; Sodium: 461mg; Carbohydrates: 69g; Fiber: 2g; Protein: 22g

English Muffin Tuna Sandwiches

PREP TIME: 8 MINUTES / COOK TIME: 5 MINUTES / SERVES 4

There probably isn't a faster recipe on the planet—unless you want to eat dry cereal! With just a few ingredients and 13 minutes, you can enjoy a substantial sandwich made from toasted English muffins, melted cheese, and a cool spicy tuna salad.

1. In a small bowl, combine the tuna, mayonnaise, mustard, lemon juice, and green onions.
2. Butter the cut side of the English muffins. Grill butter-side up in the air fryer for 2 to 4 minutes or until light golden brown. Remove the muffins from the air fryer basket.
3. Top each muffin with one slice of cheese and return to the air fryer. Grill for 2 to 4 minutes or until the cheese melts and starts to brown.
4. Remove the muffins from the air fryer, top with the tuna mixture, and serve.

....

Ingredient tip: *If you're concerned about sustainability, opt for pole-caught tuna.*

....

Per serving: Calories: 389; Total Fat: 23g; Saturated Fat: 10g; Cholesterol: 50mg; Sodium: 495mg; Carbohydrates: 25g; Fiber: 3g; Protein: 21g

390°F GRILL

FAST, FAMILY FAVORITE

1 (6-ounce) can chunk light tuna, drained

¼ cup mayonnaise

2 tablespoons mustard

1 tablespoon lemon juice

2 green onions, minced

3 English muffins, split with a fork

3 tablespoons softened butter

6 thin slices provolone or Muenster cheese

Tuna Zucchini Melts

PREP TIME: 15 MINUTES / COOK TIME: 6 MINUTES / SERVES 4

340°F GRILL

GLUTEN-FREE

4 corn tortillas

3 tablespoons softened butter

1 (6-ounce) can chunk light tuna, drained

1 cup shredded zucchini, drained by squeezing in a kitchen towel

⅓ cup mayonnaise

2 tablespoons mustard

1 cup shredded Cheddar or Colby cheese

A tuna melt is a classic diner sandwich, which is usually cooked on the grill in butter. The air fryer makes a fabulous melt sandwich with very little added fat. The zucchini provides additional color, flavor, and nutrition to this twist on a classic.

1. Spread the tortillas with the softened butter. Place in the air fryer basket and grill for 2 to 3 minutes or until the tortillas are crisp. Remove from basket and set aside.
2. In a medium bowl, combine the tuna, zucchini, mayonnaise, and mustard, and mix well.
3. Divide the tuna mixture among the toasted tortillas. Top each with some of the shredded cheese.
4. Grill in the air fryer for 2 to 4 minutes or until the tuna mixture is hot, and the cheese melts and starts to brown. Serve.

....

Ingredient tip: *You can find tuna canned in water or in oil in most grocery stores. The oil-canned tuna has a better flavor, but the water-canned variety is lower in calories. Choose chunk light tuna for the best flavor and texture.*

....

Per serving: Calories: 428; Total Fat: 30g; Saturated Fat: 13g; Cholesterol: 71mg; Sodium: 410mg; Carbohydrates: 19g; Fiber: 3g; Protein: 22g

Shrimp and Grilled Cheese Sandwiches

PREP TIME: 10 MINUTES / COOK TIME: 6 MINUTES / SERVES 4

400°F
GRILL

FAST

The air fryer lets you make grilled cheese without having to flip the sandwiches while they cook, or hover over the stove baby-sitting them. Use your favorite cheese in this easy recipe.

1. In a medium bowl, combine the cheese, shrimp, mayonnaise, and green onion, and mix well.
2. Spread this mixture on two of the slices of bread. Top with the other slices of bread to make two sandwiches. Spread the sandwiches lightly with butter.
3. Grill in the air fryer for 5 to 7 minutes or until the bread is browned and crisp and the cheese is melted. Cut in half and serve warm.

....

Substitution tip: *Instead of the shrimp in this recipe, try using canned crabmeat, chicken, or tuna. Or for a vegetarian version, leave out the shrimp and replace with 1 cup of a different type of cheese.*

....

Per serving: Calories: 276; Total Fat: 14g; Saturated Fat: 6g; Cholesterol: 115mg; Sodium: 573mg; Carbohydrates: 16g; Fiber: 2g; Protein: 22g

1¼ cups shredded Colby, Cheddar, or Havarti cheese

1 (6-ounce) can tiny shrimp, drained

3 tablespoons mayonnaise

2 tablespoons minced green onion

4 slices whole grain or whole-wheat bread

2 tablespoons softened butter

Shrimp Croquettes

PREP TIME: 12 MINUTES / COOK TIME: 8 MINUTES / SERVES 3 TO 4

390°F FRY

FAMILY FAVORITE

⅔ pound cooked
shrimp,
shelled and
deveined
1½ cups bread
crumbs,
divided
1 egg, beaten
2 tablespoon
lemon juice
2 green onions,
finely
chopped
½ teaspoon
dried basil
Pinch salt
Freshly ground
black pepper
2 tablespoons
olive oil

Croquettes are made with finely chopped meat mixed with bread crumbs and eggs, then formed into little balls or patties and deep-fried. With the air fryer you can make the guilt-free version of this decadent dish.

1. Finely chop the shrimp. Take about 1 tablespoon of the finely chopped shrimp and chop it further until it's almost a paste. Set aside.
2. In a medium bowl, combine ½ cup of the bread crumbs with the egg and lemon juice. Let stand for 5 minutes.
3. Stir the shrimp, green onions, basil, salt, and pepper into the bread crumb mixture.
4. Combine the remaining 1 cup of bread crumbs with the olive oil on a shallow plate; mix well.
5. Form the shrimp mixture into 1½-inch round balls and press firmly with your hands. Roll in the bread crumb mixture to coat.
6. Air-fry the little croquettes in batches for 6 to 8 minutes or until they are brown and crisp. Serve with cocktail sauce for dipping, if desired.

....

Ingredient tip: To devein shrimp, make a shallow cut along the back of each shrimp to expose the dark vein. Take it out with the tip of a knife or wash it out under cool running water.

....

Per serving: Calories: 330; Total Fat: 12g; Saturated Fat: 2g; Cholesterol: 201mg; Sodium: 539mg; Carbohydrates: 31g; Fiber: 2g; Protein: 24g

Dutch Pancake with Shrimp Salsa

PREP TIME: 5 MINUTES / COOK TIME: 14 MINUTES / SERVES 4

A Dutch pancake doesn't have to be sweet! This savory version satisfies for lunch, especially when you top it with a mixture of spicy salsa and tender shrimp. Moving quickly through the first few recipe steps is key to perfecting this dish.

**390°F
BAKE**

FAST

1 tablespoon
    plus
    2 teaspoons
    butter
3 eggs
½ cup flour
½ cup milk
⅛ teaspoon salt
1 cup salsa
1 cup frozen
    fully cooked
    small shrimp,
    thawed

1. Preheat the air fryer with a 6-by-6-by-2-inch pan in the basket. Add the butter and heat until it melts.
2. Quickly combine the eggs, flour, milk, and salt in a medium bowl and beat well with an eggbeater until well mixed and frothy.
3. Carefully remove the basket with the pan from the air fryer and tilt so the butter covers the bottom of the pan. Immediately pour the batter into the hot pan and put it back in the fryer.
4. Bake for 12 to 16 minutes or until the pancake is puffed and golden brown.
5. Stir together the salsa and shrimp and top the pancake with this mixture.

....

Cooking tip: *It's easy to thaw frozen fully cooked shrimp. Just put them in a colander and run cold water over the shrimp for a few minutes. Drain the shrimp, pat dry, and they're ready to use.*

....

Per serving: Calories: 213; Total Fat: 9g; Saturated Fat: 5g; Cholesterol: 198mg; Sodium: 593mg; Carbohydrates: 18g; Fiber: 2g; Protein: 14g

Steamed Scallops with Dill

PREP TIME: 5 MINUTES / COOK TIME: 4 MINUTES / SERVES 4

**390°F
STEAM**

FAST

1 pound sea
    scallops

1 tablespoon
    lemon juice

2 teaspoons
    olive oil

1 teaspoon
    dried dill

Pinch salt

Freshly ground
    black pepper

*This recipe makes for an elegant—and quick—lunch. Or increase
the number of scallops and prepare it for dinner. The scallops
release liquid as they heat, which goes into the pan below the
basket and steams the fish. Serve on toast points or over rice.*

1. Check the scallops for a small muscle attached to the side,
   and pull it off and discard it.
2. Toss the scallops with the lemon juice, olive oil, dill, salt, and
   pepper. Put into the air fryer basket.
3. Steam for 4 to 5 minutes, tossing the basket once during
   cooking time, until the scallops are just firm when tested
   with your finger. The internal temperature should be 145°F
   at minimum.

....

*Ingredient tip: There are two kinds of scallops—bay scallops and sea
scallops. They are very different sizes; one is tiny, and the other large.
Here's an easy way to remember which is which: Bay scallops are smaller,
because a bay is smaller than the sea.*

....

Per serving: Calories: 121; Total Fat: 3g; Saturated Fat: 0g; Cholesterol: 37mg; Sodium: 223mg;
Carbohydrates: 3g; Fiber: 0g; Protein: 19g

Chicken Pita Sandwiches

PREP TIME: 10 MINUTES / COOK TIME: 10 MINUTES / SERVES 4

Pita bread makes wonderful sandwiches, but if you've only used cold fillings for these little pockets, you're in for a treat. Here, chicken, onion, and bell peppers are cooked until tender then tucked into pitas with fresh veggies and dressing.

**380°F
BAKE**

FAMILY FAVORITE

2 boneless, skinless chicken breasts, cut into 1-inch cubes

1 small red onion, sliced

1 red bell pepper, sliced

⅓ cup Italian salad dressing, divided

½ teaspoon dried thyme

4 pita pockets, split

2 cups torn butter lettuce

1 cup chopped cherry tomatoes

1. Place the chicken, onion, and bell pepper in the air fryer basket. Drizzle with 1 tablespoon of the Italian salad dressing, add the thyme, and toss.
2. Bake for 9 to 11 minutes or until the chicken is 165°F on a food thermometer, tossing once during cooking time.
3. Transfer the chicken and vegetables to a bowl and toss with the remaining salad dressing.
4. Assemble sandwiches with the pita pockets, butter lettuce, and cherry tomatoes.

....

Substitution tip: *This easy recipe can be made with cubed pork tenderloin or cubed chicken thighs. Both of these meats will take a few minutes longer to cook than the chicken breasts. Cook the pork to at least 145°F and the chicken thighs to 165°F.*

....

Per serving: Calories: 414; Total Fat: 19g; Saturated Fat: 4g; Cholesterol: 101mg; Sodium: 253mg; Carbohydrates: 22g; Fiber: 2g; Protein: 36g

Chicken à la King

PREP TIME: 10 MINUTES / COOK TIME: 17 MINUTES / SERVES 4

**350°F
ROAST**

FAMILY FAVORITE

2 boneless, skin-less chicken breasts, cut into 1-inch cubes

8 button mushrooms, sliced

1 red bell pepper, chopped

1 tablespoon olive oil

1 (10-ounce) package refrigerated Alfredo sauce

½ teaspoon dried thyme

6 slices French bread

2 tablespoons softened butter

Chicken à la King is another dinner classic, but that doesn't mean you can't enjoy it for lunch. Tender chicken is cooked in a white sauce, and then the whole thing is served with crusty bread.

1. Place the chicken, mushrooms, and bell pepper in the air fryer basket. Drizzle with the olive oil and toss to coat.
2. Roast for 10 to 15 minutes or until the chicken is 165°F on a food thermometer, tossing the food once during cooking time.
3. Remove the chicken and vegetables to a 6-inch metal bowl and stir in the Alfredo sauce and thyme. Return to the air fryer and cook for 3 to 4 minutes or until hot.
4. Meanwhile, spread the French bread slices with the butter. When the chicken is done, remove the pan from the basket and add the bread, butter-side up. Toast for 2 to 4 minutes or until light golden brown.
5. Place the toast on a serving plate and top with the chicken.

....

Air Fryer tip: *If your air fryer didn't come with a pan to cook things in the basket, buy one! You can find 6-by-6-by-2-inch pans in many kitchen supply stores. And a 6-inch metal bowl will hold ingredients and mixtures that are too large for the pan. Just make sure that the bowl fits into your air fryer basket.*

....

Per serving: Calories: 744; Total Fat: 32g; Saturated Fat: 15g; Cholesterol: 142mg; Sodium: 3,904mg; Carbohydrates: 64g; Fiber: 2g; Protein: 50g

Sweet and Hot Bacon and Bell Pepper Sandwiches

PREP TIME: 15 MINUTES / COOK TIME: 7 MINUTES / SERVES 4

Precooked bacon, which you can find in the meat section of the supermarket, is a great convenience food that works beautifully in the air fryer. Because it is completely cooked, it only needs to be heated. And it releases much less fat than raw bacon, so the air fryer will not smoke.

1. In a small bowl, combine the barbecue sauce and the honey. Brush this mixture lightly onto the bacon slices and the red and yellow pepper slices.
2. Put the peppers into the air fryer basket and grill for 4 minutes. Then shake the basket, add the bacon, and grill for 2 minutes or until the bacon is browned and the peppers are tender.
3. Fill the pita halves with the bacon, peppers, any remaining barbecue sauce, lettuce, and tomatoes, and serve immediately.

....

Substitution tip: *You can use Canadian bacon instead of precooked bacon. Cut each slice of Canadian bacon into three pieces and cook as directed in the recipe.*

....

Per serving: Calories: 358; Total Fat: 17g; Saturated Fat: 5g; Cholesterol: 42mg; Sodium: 1,228mg; Carbohydrates:35g; Fiber: 3g; Protein: 17g

350°F GRILL

FAMILY FAVORITE

⅓ cup spicy barbecue sauce

2 tablespoons honey

8 slices precooked bacon, cut into thirds

1 red bell pepper, sliced

1 yellow bell pepper, sliced

3 pita pockets, cut in half

1¼ cups torn butter lettuce leaves

2 tomatoes, sliced

4

APPETIZERS

Steamed Pot Stickers

PREP TIME: 20 MINUTES / COOK TIME: 20 MINUTES /
MAKES 30 POT STICKERS

**360°F
STEAM**

**FAMILY FAVORITE,
VEGETARIAN**

½ cup finely
chopped
cabbage

¼ cup finely
chopped red
bell pepper

2 green onions,
finely
chopped

1 egg, beaten

2 tablespoons
cocktail sauce

2 teaspoons low-
sodium soy
sauce

30 wonton
wrappers

3 tablespoons
water, plus
more for
brushing the
wrappers

Pot stickers are little Chinese dumplings that you can fill with anything you want, although you'll typically find meat or veggies tucked inside. To make these vegetarian appetizers, look for wonton wrappers in the produce section of your supermarket.

1. In a small bowl, combine the cabbage, pepper, green onions, egg, cocktail sauce, and soy sauce, and mix well.
2. Put about 1 teaspoon of the mixture in the center of each wonton wrapper. Fold the wrapper in half, covering the filling; dampen the edges with water, and seal. You can crimp the edges of the wrapper with your fingers so they look like the pot stickers you get in restaurants. Brush them with water.
3. Put 3 tablespoons water in the pan under the air fryer basket. Cook the pot stickers in 2 batches for 9 to 10 minutes or until the pot stickers are hot and the bottoms are lightly browned.

Substitution tip: *Use other vegetables in this recipe, such as corn, baby peas, or chopped zucchini or summer squash. You could also add leftover cooked meat such as pork or chicken, finely chopped.*

Per serving (3 pot stickers): Calories: 291; Total Fat: 2g; Saturated Fat: 0g; Cholesterol: 35mg; Sodium: 649mg; Carbohydrates: 57g; Fiber: 3g; Protein: 10g

Beef and Mango Skewers

PREP TIME: 10 MINUTES / COOK TIME: 5 MINUTES / SERVES 4

Any kabob or skewered food cooks beautifully in the air fryer. The meat cooks up tender with a slight crust, and the fruit becomes caramelized and soft.

1. Put the beef cubes in a medium bowl and add the balsamic vinegar, olive oil, honey, marjoram, salt, and pepper. Mix well, then massage the marinade into the beef with your hands. Set aside.
2. To prepare the mango, stand it on end and cut the skin off, using a sharp knife. Then carefully cut around the oval pit to remove the flesh. Cut the mango into 1-inch cubes.
3. Thread metal skewers alternating with three beef cubes and two mango cubes.
4. Grill the skewers in the air fryer basket for 4 to 7 minutes or until the beef is browned and at least 145°F.

....

Substitution tip: *You can substitute peaches or nectarines for the mango in this recipe if you can't find a ripe mango. When gently pressed, any ripe stone fruit will give slightly and smell sweet.*

....

Per serving: Calories: 242; Total Fat: 9g; Saturated Fat: 3g; Cholesterol: 76mg; Sodium: 96mg; Carbohydrates: 13g; Fiber: 1g; Protein: 26g

390°F GRILL

FAST, GLUTEN-FREE

¾ pound beef sirloin tip, cut into 1-inch cubes
2 tablespoons balsamic vinegar
1 tablespoon olive oil
1 tablespoon honey
½ teaspoon dried marjoram
Pinch salt
Freshly ground black pepper
1 mango

Curried Sweet Potato Fries

PREP TIME: 5 MINUTES / COOK TIME: 8 TO 12 MINUTES / SERVES 4

**390°F
BAKE**

**FAST, FAMILY
FAVORITE,
GLUTEN-FREE**

½ cup sour
cream
½ cup mango
chutney
3 teaspoons
curry powder,
divided
4 cups frozen
sweet potato
fries
1 tablespoon
olive oil
Pinch salt
Freshly ground
black pepper

If you've never tried sweet potato fries, they may become your new favorite! The potatoes are crisp and tender, and when coated with butter and curry powder, they take on an irresistible flavor, especially when served with this creamy dip.

1. In a small bowl, combine sour cream, chutney, and 1½ teaspoons of the curry powder. Mix well and set aside.
2. Put the sweet potatoes in a medium bowl. Drizzle with the olive oil and sprinkle with remaining 1½ teaspoons curry powder, salt, and pepper.
3. Put the potatoes in the air fryer basket. Cook for 8 to 12 minutes or until crisp, hot, and golden brown, shaking the basket once during cooking time.
4. Place the fries in a serving basket and serve with the chutney dip.

....

Substitution tip: *You can use fresh sweet potatoes in place of the frozen precut fries. Use one or two sweet potatoes, peel them, and cut into ⅓-inch thick strips using a sharp knife or mandoline. Use as directed in recipe, but you will need to increase the cooking time.*

....

Per serving: Calories: 323; Total Fat: 10g; Saturated Fat: 4g; Cholesterol: 13mg; Sodium: 138mg; Carbohydrates: 58g; Fiber: 7g; Protein: 3g

Spicy Kale Chips with Yogurt Sauce

PREP TIME: 10 MINUTES / COOK TIME: 5 MINUTES / SERVES 4

Chips made from kale are unusual, delicious, and very good for you. This sturdy leafy green actually fries very well, considering it's high in water content. The spicy dipping sauce pairs perfectly with the crisp chips.

1. In a small bowl, combine the yogurt, lemon juice, honey mustard, and oregano, and set aside.
2. Remove the stems and ribs from the kale with a sharp knife. Cut the leaves into 2- to 3-inch pieces.
3. Toss the kale with olive oil, salt, and pepper. Massage the oil into the leaves with your hands.
4. Air-fry the kale in batches until crisp, about 5 minutes, shaking the basket once during cooking time. Serve with the yogurt sauce.

....

Ingredient tip: *Kale comes in several different varieties. Tuscan (also known as dinosaur or lacinato) kale is the sturdiest and makes excellent chips. Curly kale, the variety most widely found in grocery stores, can become slightly frizzy when cooked in the air fryer, but is still delicious.*

....

Per serving: Calories: 154; Total Fat: 8g; Saturated Fat: 2g; Cholesterol: 3mg; Sodium: 378mg; Carbohydrates: 13g; Fiber: 1g; Protein: 8g

390°F FRY

FAST, FAMILY FAVORITE, VEGETARIAN, GLUTEN-FREE

1 cup Greek yogurt
3 tablespoons lemon juice
2 tablespoons honey mustard
½ teaspoon dried oregano
1 bunch curly kale
2 tablespoons olive oil
½ teaspoon salt
⅛ teaspoon pepper

Phyllo Artichoke Triangles

PREP TIME: 15 MINUTES / COOK TIME: 10 MINUTES / MAKES 18 TRIANGLES

**400°F
BAKE**

VEGETARIAN

¼ cup ricotta cheese

1 egg white

⅓ cup minced drained artichoke hearts

3 tablespoons grated mozzarella cheese

½ teaspoon dried thyme

6 sheets frozen phyllo dough, thawed

2 tablespoons melted butter

A creamy filling is wrapped in crisp phyllo dough, then baked until brown and crunchy. Your guests will love this classic. If you want more spice, make this recipe with marinated artichoke hearts.

1. In a small bowl, combine ricotta cheese, egg white, artichoke hearts, mozzarella cheese, and thyme, and mix well.
2. Cover the phyllo dough with a damp kitchen towel while you work so it doesn't dry out. Using one sheet at a time, place on the work surface and cut into thirds lengthwise.
3. Put about 1½ teaspoons of the filling on each strip at the base. Fold the bottom right-hand tip of phyllo over the filling to meet the other side in a triangle, then continue folding in a triangle. Brush each triangle with butter to seal the edges. Repeat with remaining phyllo dough and filling.
4. Bake, 6 at a time, for about 3 to 4 minutes or until the phyllo is golden brown and crisp.

....

Substitution tip: *You can use anything in this filling in place of the artichoke hearts. Try spinach, chopped cooked shrimp, cooked sausage, or keep it vegetarian and use all grated cheese.*

....

Per serving (3 triangles): Calories: 271; Total Fat: 17g; Saturated Fat: 7g; Cholesterol: 19mg; Sodium: 232mg; Carbohydrates: 23g; Fiber: 5g; Protein: 9g

Spinach Dip with Bread Knots

PREP TIME: 12 MINUTES / COOK TIME: 16 TO 21 MINUTES / SERVES 6

This wonderful appetizer features a creamy hot spinach dip topped with knots made out of breadstick dough. To serve, put the pan out on a trivet so your guests can pull off the bread knots and sop up the dip!

1. Spray a 6-by-6-by-2-inch pan with nonstick cooking spray.
2. In a medium bowl, combine the cream cheese, sour cream, spinach, Swiss cheese, and green onions, and mix well. Spread into the prepared pan and bake for 8 minutes or until hot.
3. While the dip is baking, unroll six of the breadsticks and cut them in half crosswise to make 12 pieces.
4. Gently stretch each piece of dough and tie into a loose knot; tuck in the ends.
5. When the dip is hot, remove from the air fryer and carefully place each bread knot on top of the dip, covering the surface of the dip. Brush each knot with melted butter and sprinkle Parmesan cheese on top.
6. Bake for 8 to 13 minutes or until the bread knots are golden brown and cooked through.

....

Ingredient tip: *After the dip is done and eaten, you can coat the remaining breadstick dough pieces in butter and cheese and bake in the air fryer at 300°F for about half the time recommended on the package. Serve with soup or freeze them to enjoy later.*

....

Per serving: Calories: 264; Total Fat: 23g; Saturated Fat: 14g; Cholesterol: 68mg; Sodium: 270mg; Carbohydrates: 7g; Fiber: 0g; Protein: 8g

320°F BAKE

VEGETARIAN

Nonstick cooking spray
1 (8-ounce) package cream cheese, cut into cubes
¼ cup sour cream
½ cup frozen chopped spinach, thawed and drained
½ cup grated Swiss cheese
2 green onions, chopped
½ (11-ounce) can refrigerated breadstick dough
2 tablespoons melted butter
3 tablespoons grated Parmesan cheese

Arancini

PREP TIME: 15 MINUTES / COOK TIME: 16 TO 22 MINUTES / MAKES 16 ARANCINI

400°F FRY

FAMILY FAVORITE, VEGETARIAN

2 cups cooked and cooled rice or leftover risotto

2 eggs, beaten

1½ cups panko bread crumbs, divided

½ cup grated Parmesan cheese

2 tablespoons minced fresh basil

16 ¾-inch cubes mozzarella cheese

2 tablespoons olive oil

Popular in Italy, arancini *are little balls of rice that are sometimes stuffed with cheese or another savory filling and deep fried. You can use leftover risotto to make this recipe, or use leftover rice from your local Chinese restaurant.*

1. In a medium bowl, combine the rice, eggs, ½ cup of the bread crumbs, Parmesan cheese, and basil. Form this mixture into 16 1½-inch balls.
2. Poke a hole in each of the balls with your finger and insert a mozzarella cube. Form the rice mixture firmly around the cheese.
3. On a shallow plate, combine the remaining 1 cup bread crumbs with the olive oil and mix well. Roll the rice balls in the bread crumbs to coat.
4. Cook the arancini in batches for 8 to 11 minutes or until golden brown.

....

Did You Know? *In Italy,* arancini, *also called* supplì *or rice frittata, are sold on the street as a snack food. They are made much bigger in that country, about the size of an orange, and are often formed into a cone shape.*

....

Per serving (2 arancini): Calories: 378; Total Fat: 11g; Saturated Fat: 4g; Cholesterol: 57mg; Sodium: 361mg; Carbohydrates: 53g; Fiber: 2g; Protein: 16g

Pesto Bruschetta

PREP TIME: 10 MINUTES / COOK TIME: 4 TO 8 MINUTES / SERVES 4

A classic Italian sauce, pesto is made with fresh basil, olive oil, garlic, and Parmesan cheese. Here, the bright and assertive sauce is mixed with fresh tomatoes and slathered onto warm, crisp cheese bread.

350°F BAKE

FAST, VEGETARIAN

1. Spread the bread with the butter and place butter-side up in the air fryer basket. Bake for 3 to 5 minutes or until the bread is light golden brown.
2. Remove the bread from the basket and top each piece with some of the cheese. Return to the basket in batches and bake until the cheese melts, about 1 to 3 minutes.
3. Meanwhile, combine the pesto, tomatoes, and green onions in a small bowl.
4. When the cheese has melted, remove the bread from the air fryer and place on a serving plate. Top each slice with some of the pesto mixture and serve.

8 slices French bread, ½ inch thick

2 tablespoons softened butter

1 cup shredded mozzarella cheese

½ cup basil pesto

1 cup chopped grape tomatoes

2 green onions, thinly sliced

....

Ingredient tip: *You can find basil pesto and other types of pesto, including a sauce made from sun-dried tomatoes, in the refrigerated section or the pasta aisle of any supermarket.*

....

Per serving: Calories: 462; Total Fat: 25g; Saturated Fat: 10g; Cholesterol: 38mg; Sodium: 822mg; Carbohydrates: 41g; Fiber: 3g; Protein: 19g

Fried Tortellini with Spicy Dipping Sauce

PREP TIME: 8 MINUTES / COOK TIME: 20 MINUTES / SERVES 4

380°F FRY

FAMILY FAVORITE, VEGETARIAN

¾ cup mayonnaise

2 tablespoons mustard

1 egg

½ cup flour

½ teaspoon dried oregano

1½ cups bread crumbs

2 tablespoons olive oil

2 cups frozen cheese tortellini

Did you know that you can fry tortellini to produce a fancy appetizer? Frozen tortellini can be found in most supermarkets in the freezer section. Serve with a spicy tomato sauce for dipping.

1. In a small bowl, combine the mayonnaise and mustard and mix well. Set aside.
2. In a shallow bowl, beat the egg. In a separate bowl, combine the flour and oregano. In another bowl, combine the bread crumbs and olive oil, and mix well.
3. Drop the tortellini, a few at a time, into the egg, then into the flour, then into the egg again, and then into the bread crumbs to coat. Put into the air fryer basket, cooking in batches.
4. Air-fry for about 10 minutes, shaking halfway through the cooking time, or until the tortellini are crisp and golden brown on the outside. Serve with the mayonnaise.

Substitution tip: *You can also cook ravioli or even pierogies, which are large Eastern European dumplings, this way. The ravioli will take about 15 minutes to cook, and the pierogies about 20 minutes, until hot.*

Per serving: Calories: 698; Total Fat: 31g; Saturated Fat: 4g; Cholesterol: 66mg; Sodium: 832mg; Carbohydrates: 88g; Fiber: 3g; Protein: 18g

Shrimp Toast

PREP TIME: 15 MINUTES / COOK TIME: 6 TO 12 MINUTES / MAKES 12 TOASTS

Shrimp toast is a classic appetizer popular in Chinese restaurants. In the traditional preparation, chopped shrimp is mixed with egg whites and seasonings and spread on toast, then deep-fried until crisp. The air fryer makes this recipe a breeze because you don't have to mess with hot oil and turning the little toasts as they cook.

350°F FRY

FAMILY FAVORITE

3 slices firm white bread

⅔ cup finely chopped peeled and deveined raw shrimp

1 egg white

2 cloves garlic, minced

2 tablespoons cornstarch

¼ teaspoon ground ginger

Pinch salt

Freshly ground black pepper

2 tablespoons olive oil

1. Cut the crusts from the bread using a sharp knife; crumble the crusts to make bread crumbs. Set aside.
2. In a small bowl, combine the shrimp, egg white, garlic, cornstarch, ginger, salt, and pepper, and mix well.
3. Spread the shrimp mixture evenly on the bread to the edges. With a sharp knife, cut each slice into 4 strips.
4. Mix the bread crumbs with the olive oil and pat onto the shrimp mixture. Place the shrimp toasts in the air fryer basket in a single layer; you may need to cook in batches.
5. Air-fry for 3 to 6 minutes, until crisp and golden brown.

Substitution tip: *Substitute finely minced cooked crabmeat for the shrimp in this recipe, or use ground chicken or ground turkey instead.*

Per serving (2 toasts): Calories: 121; Total Fat: 6g; Saturated Fat: 1g; Cholesterol: 72mg; Sodium: 158mg; Carbohydrates: 7g; Fiber: 0g; Protein: 9g

Bacon Tater Tots

PREP TIME: 5 MINUTES / COOK TIME: 17 MINUTES / SERVES 4

400°F FRY

FAMILY FAVORITE, GLUTEN-FREE

24 frozen
   tater tots
6 slices
   precooked
   bacon
2 tablespoons
   maple syrup
1 cup shredded
   Cheddar
   cheese

This recipe is a perfect snack for tailgating before the big game! The combination of potatoes and bacon with cheese is the ultimate comfort food.

1. Put the tater tots in the air fryer basket. Air-fry for 10 minutes, shaking the basket halfway through the cooking time.
2. Meanwhile, cut the bacon into 1-inch pieces and shred the cheese.
3. Remove the tater tots from the air fryer basket and put into a 6-by-6-by-2-inch pan. Top with the bacon and drizzle with the maple syrup. Air-fry for 5 minutes or until the tots and bacon are crisp.
4. Top with the cheese and air-fry for 2 minutes or until the cheese is melted.

....

Ingredient tip: *Only use the precooked bacon that doesn't need refrigeration for this recipe. If you use regular bacon, it will give off too much fat and the tater tots will end up soggy, not crisp.*

....

Per serving: Calories: 374; Total Fat: 22g; Saturated Fat: 9g; Cholesterol: 40mg; Sodium: 857mg; Carbohydrates: 34g; Fiber: 2g; Protein: 13g

Hash Brown Bruschetta

PREP TIME: 7 MINUTES / COOK TIME: 6 TO 8 MINUTES / SERVES 4

Bruschetta, of Italian origin, is made of crisp toast piled with ingredients such as chopped tomatoes and herbs. In this recipe, crisp hash brown patties stand in for the toast. Frozen hash brown patties cook perfectly in the air fryer, with very little fat!

1. Place the hash brown patties in the air fryer in a single layer. Air-fry for 6 to 8 minutes or until the potatoes are crisp, hot, and golden brown.
2. Meanwhile, combine the olive oil, tomatoes, mozzarella, Parmesan, vinegar, and basil in a small bowl.
3. When the potatoes are done, carefully remove from the basket and arrange on a serving plate. Top with the tomato mixture and serve.

....

Did You Know? *Bruschetta comes from the word that means "to roast over coals," and refers to the toasted bread. It has many incarnations, including a recipe made by simply rubbing the warm little toasts with a cut clove of fresh garlic.*

....

Per serving: Calories: 123; Total Fat: 6g; Saturated Fat: 2g; Cholesterol: 6mg; Sodium: 81mg; Carbohydrates: 14g; Fiber: 2g; Protein: 5g

400°F FRY

FAST, FAMILY FAVORITE, VEGETARIAN, GLUTEN-FREE

4 frozen hash brown patties

1 tablespoon olive oil

⅓ cup chopped cherry tomatoes

3 tablespoons diced fresh mozzarella

2 tablespoons grated Parmesan cheese

1 tablespoon balsamic vinegar

1 tablespoon minced fresh basil

Waffle Fry Poutine

PREP TIME: 10 MINUTES / COOK TIME: 15 TO 17 MINUTES / SERVES 4

380°F
FRY
———

FAMILY FAVORITE

2 cups frozen
waffle cut
fries

2 teaspoons
olive oil

1 red bell
pepper,
chopped

2 green onions,
sliced

1 cup shredded
Swiss cheese

½ cup bottled
chicken gravy

Poutine is a traditional French Canadian recipe of fries topped with cheese curds and beef gravy. Of course, cooking it in the air fryer helps cut the calories. Other healthy upgrades include using grated cheese, chicken gravy, and incorporating veggies!

1. Toss the waffle fries with olive oil and place in the air fryer basket. Air-fry for 10 to 12 minutes or until the fries are crisp and light golden brown, shaking the basket halfway through the cooking time.
2. Transfer the fries to a 6-by-6-by-2-inch pan and top with the pepper, green onions, and cheese. Air-fry for 3 minutes until the vegetables are crisp and tender.
3. Remove the pan from the air fryer and drizzle the gravy over the fries. Air-fry for 2 minutes or until the gravy is hot. Serve immediately.

···

Substitution tip: *You can make this recipe with regular frozen French fries as well, but those may take a few minutes longer to cook. Use your favorite cheese in this hearty recipe.*

···

Per serving: Calories: 347; Total Fat: 19g; Saturated Fat: 7g; Cholesterol: 26mg; Sodium: 435mg; Carbohydrates: 33g; Fiber: 4g; Protein: 12g

Crispy Beef Cubes

PREP TIME: 10 MINUTES / COOK TIME: 12 TO 16 MINUTES / SERVES 4

Beef cooks beautifully in the air fryer. This unusual method of dipping the beef in a cheese sauce and rolling it in bread crumbs makes a crisp little mouthful with tender and juicy insides.

1. In a medium bowl, toss the beef with the pasta sauce to coat.
2. In a shallow bowl, combine the bread crumbs, oil, and marjoram, and mix well. Drop the beef cubes, one at a time, into the bread crumb mixture to coat thoroughly.
3. Cook the beef in two batches for 6 to 8 minutes, shaking the basket once during cooking time, until the beef is at least 145°F and the outside is crisp and brown. Serve with toothpicks or little forks.

....

Cooking tip: *You can use the remaining pasta sauce to make a quick lunch. Just cook a cup or two of pasta while you heat the sauce in a saucepan. Combine and enjoy.*

....

Per serving: Calories: 554; Total Fat: 22g; Saturated Fat: 8g; Cholesterol: 112mg; Sodium: 1,832mg; Carbohydrates: 43g; Fiber: 2g; Protein: 44g

360°F BAKE

FAMILY FAVORITE

1 pound sirloin tip, cut into 1-inch cubes

1 cup cheese pasta sauce (from a 16-ounce jar)

1½ cups soft bread crumbs

2 tablespoons olive oil

½ teaspoon dried marjoram

Buffalo Chicken Bites

PREP TIME: 10 MINUTES / COOK TIME: 14 TO 18 MINUTES / SERVES 4

These little bites are packed full of flavor. The tender chicken is enveloped in a spicy sauce, then coated with crisp bread crumbs. A cool dipping sauce provides the perfect accompaniment.

**350°F
FRY**

FAMILY FAVORITE

⅔ cup sour cream

¼ cup creamy blue cheese salad dressing

¼ cup crumbled blue cheese

1 celery stalk, finely chopped

1 pound chicken tenders, cut into thirds crosswise

3 tablespoons Buffalo chicken wing sauce

1 cup panko bread crumbs

2 tablespoons olive oil

1. In a small bowl, combine the sour cream, salad dressing, blue cheese, and celery, and set aside.
2. In a medium bowl, combine the chicken pieces and Buffalo wing sauce and stir to coat. Let sit while you get the bread crumbs ready.
3. Combine the bread crumbs and olive oil on a plate and mix.
4. Coat the chicken pieces in the bread crumb mixture, patting each piece so the crumbs adhere.
5. Air-fry in batches for 7 to 9 minutes, shaking the basket once, until the chicken is cooked to 165°F and is golden brown. Serve with the blue cheese sauce on the side.

....

Did You Know? *Buffalo chicken wings were first invented in the Anchor Bar in Buffalo, New York, when the owner needed to serve a lot of appetizers in a hurry. They became an immediate hit and the flavor—a combination of a spicy hot sauce with cool blue cheese—is now a classic.*

....

Per serving: Calories: 467; Total Fat: 23g; Saturated Fat: 8g; Cholesterol: 119mg; Sodium: 821mg; Carbohydrates: 22g; Fiber: 1g; Protein: 43g

Sweet and Hot Chicken Wings

PREP TIME: 5 MINUTES / COOK TIME: 25 MINUTES / MAKES 16 WINGS

Chicken wings make a great appetizer during a big game or when you're grilling outside. The air fryer makes the wings crispy and tender, and the sweet and hot sauce provides the perfect finishing touch.

**390°F
BAKE**

FAMILY FAVORITE

8 chicken wings

1 tablespoon olive oil

⅓ cup brown sugar

2 tablespoons honey

⅓ cup apple cider vinegar

2 cloves garlic, minced

½ teaspoon dried red pepper flakes

¼ teaspoon salt

1. Cut each chicken wing into three pieces. You'll have one large piece, one medium piece, and one small end. Discard the small end or save it for stock.
2. In a medium bowl, toss the wings with the oil. Transfer to the air fryer basket and cook for 20 minutes, shaking the basket twice while cooking.
3. Meanwhile, in a small bowl, combine the sugar, honey, vinegar, red pepper flakes, garlic, and salt, and whisk until combined.
4. Remove the wings from the air fryer basket and put into a 6-by-6-by-2-inch pan. Pour the sauce over the wings and toss.
5. Return to the air fryer and cook for 5 minutes or until the wings are glazed.

....

Ingredient tip: *You can sometimes buy "chicken drummettes" in the meat section. They are made from the meaty part of the chicken wing. If you want to use those instead of the cut-up whole wings, use about 10 in this recipe.*

....

Per serving (4 wings): Calories: 438; Total Fat: 16g; Saturated Fat: 4g; Cholesterol: 151mg; Sodium: 299mg; Carbohydrates: 21g; Fiber: 0g; Protein: 49g

5

FISH AND SEAFOOD

6

POULTRY

Roasted Veggie Chicken Salad

PREP TIME: 10 MINUTES / COOK TIME: 10 TO 13 MINUTES / SERVES 4

400°F
ROAST

**FAMILY FAVORITE,
GLUTEN-FREE**

3 boneless, skin-
less chicken
breasts, cut
into 1-inch
cubes

1 small red
onion, sliced

1 orange bell
pepper, sliced

1 cup sliced
yellow
summer
squash

4 tablespoons
honey
mustard salad
dressing,
divided

½ teaspoon
dried thyme

½ cup
mayonnaise

2 tablespoons
lemon juice

Have you ever eaten a warm chicken salad? It has more flavor than chicken salad served cold, and is much quicker to prepare. This one is full of colorful ingredients.

1. Place the chicken, onion, pepper, and squash in the air fryer basket. Drizzle with 1 tablespoon of the honey mustard salad dressing, add the thyme, and toss.
2. Roast for 10 to 13 minutes or until the chicken is 165°F on a food thermometer, tossing the food once during cooking time.
3. Transfer the chicken and vegetables to a bowl and mix in the remaining 3 tablespoons of honey mustard salad dressing, the mayonnaise, and lemon juice. Serve on lettuce leaves, if desired.

....

Variation tip: *You can let this salad cool down and use it as a filling for chicken salad sandwiches. Use ciabatta rolls, croissants, or pita bread.*

....

Per serving: Calories: 494; Total Fat: 23g; Saturated Fat: 5g; Cholesterol: 159mg; Sodium: 439mg; Carbohydrates: 18g; Fiber: 2g; Protein: 51g

Asian Turkey Meatballs

PREP TIME: 10 MINUTES / COOK TIME: 20 TO 24 MINUTES / SERVES 4

The Asian flavors make these turkey meatballs sing. To make tender meatballs, combine all of the ingredients then add the meat last.

1. In a 6-by-6-by-2-inch pan, combine the peanut oil and onion. Cook for 1 to 2 minutes or until crisp and tender. Transfer the onions to a medium bowl.
2. Add the water chestnuts, ground ginger, soy sauce, and bread crumbs to the onions and mix well. Add egg and stir well. Mix in the ground turkey until combined.
3. Form the mixture into 1-inch meatballs. Drizzle the remaining 1 tablespoon of oil over the meatballs.
4. Bake the meatballs in the 6-by-6-by-2-inch pan in batches for 10 to 12 minutes or until they are 165°F on a meat thermometer.

....

Variation tip: *You can add a sauce if you'd like. Combine 2 tablespoons cornstarch, 1 cup chicken broth, and ½ cup pineapple juice. Put the meatballs in a 6-inch bowl and add the sauce. Bake the mixture for 4 to 6 minutes, or until the sauce has thickened. Serve over hot rice.*

....

Per serving: Calories: 336; Total Fat: 21g; Saturated Fat: 4g; Cholesterol: 157mg; Sodium: 487mg; Carbohydrates: 8g; Fiber: 1g; Protein: 34g

400°F BAKE

FAMILY FAVORITE

2 tablespoons peanut oil, divided

1 small onion, minced

¼ cup water chestnuts, finely chopped

½ teaspoon ground ginger

2 tablespoons low-sodium soy sauce

¼ cup panko bread crumbs

1 egg, beaten

1 pound ground turkey

Stir-Fried Chicken with Pineapple

PREP TIME: 10 MINUTES / COOK TIME: 11 TO 15 MINUTES / SERVES 4

FAMILY FAVORITE

2 boneless, skin-
less chicken
breasts

2 tablespoons
cornstarch

1 egg white,
lightly beaten

1 tablespoon
olive or
peanut oil

1 onion, sliced

1 red bell
pepper,
chopped

1 (8-ounce) can
pineapple
tidbits,
drained, juice
reserved

2 tablespoons
reduced-
sodium soy
sauce

Stir-fried chicken is usually coated with a mixture of cornstarch and egg white. This technique is called "velveting" and it makes chicken that is exceptionally tender. The chicken is combined with onion and pineapple in this easy recipe. Serve over hot rice.

1. Cut the chicken breasts into cubes and put into a medium bowl. Add the cornstarch and egg white and mix together thoroughly. Set aside.

2. In a 6-inch metal bowl, combine the oil and the onion. Cook in the air fryer for 2 to 3 minutes or until the onion is crisp and tender.

3. Drain the chicken and add to the bowl with the onions; stir well. Cook for 7 to 9 minutes or until the chicken is thoroughly cooked to 165°F.

4. Stir the chicken mixture, then add the pepper, pineapple tidbits, 3 tablespoons of the reserved pineapple liquid, and the soy sauce, and stir again. Cook for 2 to 3 minutes or until the food is cooked and the sauce is slightly thickened.

Substitution tip: *You can use boneless, skinless chicken thighs in this recipe in place of the chicken breasts. Cook the thighs for 8 to 10 minutes until the chicken is 165°F on a meat thermometer.*

Per serving: Calories: 291; Total Fat: 9g; Saturated Fat: 2g; Cholesterol: 101mg; Sodium: 427mg; Carbohydrates: 16g; Fiber: 2g; Protein: 35g

Sweet-and-Sour Drumsticks

PREP TIME: 5 MINUTES / COOK TIME: 23 TO 25 MINUTES / SERVES 4

Cooking chicken drumsticks in the air fryer is a two-part process: The meat is first cooked until done, then coated with a sweet-and-sour sauce and cooked until glazed. The extra step creates an extra special dish.

1. Sprinkle the drumsticks with 1 tablespoon of lemon juice and 1 tablespoon of soy sauce. Place in the air fryer basket and drizzle with the peanut oil. Toss to coat. Bake for 18 minutes or until the chicken is almost done.
2. Meanwhile, in a 6-inch bowl combine the remaining 2 tablespoons of lemon juice, the remaining 2 tablespoons of soy sauce, honey, brown sugar, ketchup, and pineapple juice.
3. Add the cooked chicken to the bowl and stir to coat the chicken well with the sauce.
4. Place the metal bowl in the basket. Cook for 5 to 7 minutes or until the chicken is glazed and registers 165°F on a meat thermometer.

....

Substitution tip: *You can cook boneless, skinless chicken breasts or thighs using this method. Reduce the cooking time to 10 to 15 minutes for the chicken breasts and 11 to 16 minutes for the chicken thighs.*

....

Per serving: Calories: 242; Total Fat: 7g; Saturated Fat: 2g; Cholesterol: 61mg; Sodium: 804mg; Carbohydrates: 25g; Fiber: 0g; Protein: 20g

350°F BAKE

FAMILY FAVORITE

6 chicken drumsticks

3 tablespoons lemon juice, divided

3 tablespoons low-sodium soy sauce, divided

1 tablespoon peanut oil

3 tablespoons honey

3 tablespoons brown sugar

2 tablespoons ketchup

¼ cup pineapple juice

Chicken Satay

PREP TIME: 12 MINUTES / COOK TIME: 12 TO 18 MINUTES / SERVES 4

390°F GRILL

FAMILY FAVORITE

½ cup crunchy peanut butter

⅓ cup chicken broth

3 tablespoons low-sodium soy sauce

2 tablespoons lemon juice

2 cloves garlic, minced

2 tablespoons olive oil

1 teaspoon curry powder

1 pound chicken tenders

Satay is an Indonesian dish made of meat, usually chicken, that is skewered and grilled with a spicy peanut sauce. The grilled skewers are then served with additional peanut sauce for dipping.

1. In a medium bowl, combine the peanut butter, chicken broth, soy sauce, lemon juice, garlic, olive oil, and curry powder, and mix well with a wire whisk until smooth. Remove 2 table-spoons of this mixture to a small bowl. Put remaining sauce into a serving bowl and set aside.

2. Add the chicken tenders to the bowl with the 2 tablespoons sauce and stir to coat. Let stand for a few minutes to mari-nate, then run a bamboo skewer through each chicken tender lengthwise.

3. Put the chicken in the air fryer basket and cook in batches for 6 to 9 minutes or until the chicken reaches 165°F on a meat thermometer. Serve the chicken with the reserved sauce.

Air Fryer tip: *The air fryer may smoke a bit as some of the sauce drips off the chicken. You can add a tablespoon or two of water to the pan attached to the basket if you'd like to reduce smoke.*

Per serving: Calories: 448; Total Fat: 28g; Saturated Fat: 5g; Cholesterol: 97mg; Sodium: 1,004mg; Carbohydrates: 8g; Fiber: 2g; Protein: 46g

Orange Curried Chicken Stir-Fry

PREP TIME: 10 MINUTES / COOK TIME: 16 TO 19 MINUTES / SERVES 4

This easy stir-fry recipe is flavored with orange juice and curry powder, so it's sweet and spicy. For a tasty, quick dinner, serve over hot cooked rice, along with a green salad.

**370°F
STIR-FRY**

**FAMILY FAVORITE,
GLUTEN-FREE**

1. Put the chicken thighs, pepper, and red onion in the air fryer basket and mist with olive oil.
2. Cook for 12 to 14 minutes or until the chicken is cooked to 165°F, shaking the basket halfway through cooking time.
3. Remove the chicken and vegetables from the air fryer basket and set aside.
4. In a 6-inch metal bowl, combine the stock, honey, orange juice, cornstarch, and curry powder, and mix well. Add the chicken and vegetables, stir, and put the bowl in the basket.
5. Return the basket to the air fryer and cook for 2 minutes. Remove and stir, then cook for 2 to 3 minutes or until the sauce is thickened and bubbly.

¾ pound boneless, skinless chicken thighs, cut into 1-inch pieces

1 yellow bell pepper, cut into 1½-inch pieces

1 small red onion, sliced

Olive oil for misting

¼ cup chicken stock

2 tablespoons honey

¼ cup orange juice

1 tablespoon cornstarch

2 to 3 teaspoons curry powder

....

Did You Know? *Curry powder isn't one single spice, but a combination of many spices. In India, each family makes their own unique blend.*

....

Per serving: Calories: 230; Total Fat: 7g; Saturated Fat: 2g; Cholesterol: 76mg; Sodium: 124mg; Carbohydrates: 16g; Fiber: 2g; Protein: 26g

Spicy Chicken Stir-Fry

PREP TIME: 10 MINUTES / COOK TIME: 13 TO 16 MINUTES / SERVES 4

370°F STIR-FRY

GLUTEN-FREE

2 boneless, skinless chicken breasts

2 tablespoons cornstarch

2 tablespoons peanut oil

1 onion, sliced

1 jalapeño pepper, sliced

1 red bell pepper, chopped

1 cup frozen corn

½ cup salsa

A stir-fry doesn't have to taste Asian! This colorful and fun recipe uses spicy Tex-Mex flavors to create a dinner that's ready in minutes.

1. Cut the chicken breasts into 1-inch cubes. Put the cornstarch on a shallow plate and toss the chicken in it to coat. Set the chicken aside.

2. In a 6-inch metal bowl, combine the oil and onion. Cook for 2 to 3 minutes or until crisp and tender.

3. Add the chicken to the bowl. Cook for 7 to 8 minutes or until almost cooked. Stir in the jalapeño pepper, red bell pepper, corn, and salsa.

4. Cook for 4 to 5 minutes or until the chicken is cooked to 165°F and the vegetables are crisp and tender. Serve over hot rice.

....

Ingredient tip: *Salsa can be mild or hot, depending on the type of peppers it contains. The hotter peppers are habanero and serrano. Jalapeño peppers are milder. Read labels carefully to make sure you are buying the strength of salsa you prefer.*

....

Per serving: Calories: 351; Total Fat: 16g; Saturated Fat: 4g; Cholesterol: 101mg; Sodium: 296mg; Carbohydrates: 18g; Fiber: 3g; Protein: 35g

Chicken Fajitas

PREP TIME: 10 MINUTES / COOK TIME: 10 TO 14 MINUTES / SERVES 4

Fajitas are made with grilled chicken and veggies, tossed with a spicy dressing and served with avocados and lettuce in a soft corn tortilla. You can adjust the heat of this dish with the spice level of the salsa you choose.

380°F
GRILL

**FAMILY FAVORITE,
GLUTEN-FREE**

1. Place the chicken, onion, and peppers in the air fryer basket. Drizzle with 1 tablespoon of the salad dressing and add the oregano. Toss to combine.
2. Grill for 10 to 14 minutes or until the chicken is 165°F on a food thermometer.
3. Transfer the chicken and vegetables to a bowl and toss with the remaining salad dressing.
4. Serve the chicken mixture with the tortillas, lettuce, and avocados and let everyone make their own creations.

4 boneless, skinless chicken breasts, sliced
1 small red onion, sliced
2 red bell peppers, sliced
½ cup spicy ranch salad dressing, divided
½ teaspoon dried oregano
8 corn tortillas
2 cups torn butter lettuce
2 avocados, peeled and chopped

Substitution tip: *You could use sliced boneless, skinless chicken thighs instead of the chicken breasts in this recipe. The cooking time will be a bit longer: 12 to 17 minutes. Make sure you check the doneness with a meat thermometer.*

Per serving: Calories: 783; Total Fat: 38g; Saturated Fat: 9g; Cholesterol: 202mg; Sodium: 397mg; Carbohydrates: 39g; Fiber: 12g; Protein: 72g

Tex-Mex Turkey Burgers

PREP TIME: 10 MINUTES / COOK TIME: 14 TO 16 MINUTES / SERVES 4

330°F GRILL

FAMILY FAVORITE, GLUTEN-FREE

⅓ cup finely crushed corn tortilla chips
1 egg, beaten
¼ cup salsa
⅓ cup shredded pepper Jack cheese
Pinch salt
Freshly ground black pepper
1 pound ground turkey
1 tablespoon olive oil
1 teaspoon paprika

Turkey burgers are lower in fat than burgers made from ground beef. But for food safety reasons, they must be cooked until well done, to 165°F. In this recipe, bland turkey is made memorable with offbeat flavors!

1. In a medium bowl, combine the tortilla chips, egg, salsa, cheese, salt, and pepper, and mix well.
2. Add the turkey and mix gently but thoroughly with clean hands.
3. Form the meat mixture into patties about ½ inch thick. Make an indentation in the center of each patty with your thumb so the burgers don't puff up while cooking.
4. Brush the patties on both sides with the olive oil and sprinkle with paprika.
5. Put in the air fryer basket. Grill for 14 to 16 minutes or until the meat registers at least 165°F.

Substitution tip: *You can make this recipe with ground chicken or ground pork if you'd like. Either would work well with the flavors and textures.*

Per serving: Calories: 354; Total Fat: 21g; Saturated Fat: 5g; Cholesterol: 166mg; Sodium: 337mg; Carbohydrates: 11g; Fiber: 2g; Protein: 36g

Barbecued Chicken Thighs

PREP TIME: 10 MINUTES / COOK TIME: 15 TO 18 MINUTES / SERVES 4

There are many wonderful barbecue sauces, but even the best ones can use a little more oomph. Do a taste test with a few brands and see which one you like best. They can be spicy or mellow, sweet or hot, thick or thin. Then punch up the flavor with such ingredients as garlic, herbs, or spices.

1. In a medium bowl, combine the chicken, barbecue sauce, garlic, and lemon juice, and mix well. Let marinate for 10 minutes.
2. Remove the chicken thighs from the bowl and shake off excess sauce. Put the chicken pieces in the air fryer, leaving a bit of space between each one.
3. Grill for 15 to 18 minutes or until the chicken is 165°F on an instant-read meat thermometer.

....

Air Fryer tip: *Because the sauce will drip off the chicken as it cooks, the air fryer may smoke a bit. That's okay; just check the chicken about half-way through the cooking time to make sure it isn't burning.*

....

Per serving: Calories: 351; Total Fat: 13g; Saturated Fat: 4g; Cholesterol: 151mg; Sodium: 323mg; Carbohydrates: 6g; Fiber: 0g; Protein: 49g

380°F GRILL

FAMILY FAVORITE, GLUTEN-FREE

6 boneless, skin-less chicken thighs
¼ cup store-bought gluten-free barbecue sauce
2 cloves garlic, minced
2 tablespoons lemon juice

Buttermilk Fried Chicken

PREP TIME: 15 MINUTES / COOK TIME: 20 TO 25 MINUTES / SERVES 4

**370°F
FRY**

FAMILY FAVORITE

6 chicken pieces:
   drumsticks,
   breasts, and
   thighs
1 cup flour
2 teaspoons
   paprika
Pinch salt
Freshly ground
   black pepper
⅓ cup buttermilk
2 eggs
2 tablespoons
   olive oil
1½ cups bread
   crumbs

Fried chicken is perhaps the most decadent of fried foods. But many people don't make it at home because oil splatters everywhere when you fry chicken. And it's just not healthy to eat it too often. The air fryer comes to the rescue with this wonderful adaptation.

1. Pat the chicken dry. In a shallow bowl, combine the flour, paprika, salt, and pepper.
2. In another bowl, beat the buttermilk with the eggs until smooth.
3. In a third bowl, combine the olive oil and bread crumbs until mixed.
4. Dredge the chicken in the flour, then into the eggs to coat, and finally into the bread crumbs, patting the crumbs firmly onto the chicken skin.
5. Air-fry the chicken for 20 to 25 minutes, turning each piece over halfway during cooking, until the meat registers 165°F on a meat thermometer and the chicken is brown and crisp. Let cool for 5 minutes, then serve.

....

Variation tip: You can marinate the chicken in buttermilk and spices such as cayenne pepper, chili powder, or garlic powder overnight before you cook it. This makes the chicken even more moist and tender and adds flavor.

....

Per serving: Calories: 644; Total Fat: 17g; Saturated Fat: 4g; Cholesterol: 214mg; Sodium: 495mg; Carbohydrates: 55g; Fiber: 3g; Protein: 62g

Garlic-Roasted Chicken with Creamer Potatoes

PREP TIME: 10 MINUTES / COOK TIME: 25 MINUTES / SERVES 4

Yes, you can roast a whole chicken in the air fryer, as long as it fits easily into the air fryer basket. For this recipe, choose a small broiler-fryer, about 3 pounds. It takes a little longer than 30 minutes from start to finish, but that's so the chicken will become very crisp on the outside and moist and tender on the inside.

1. **Do not wash the chicken before cooking.** Remove it from its packaging and pat the chicken dry.
2. Combine the olive oil and garlic salt in a small bowl. Rub half of this mixture on the inside of the chicken, under the skin, and on the chicken skin. Place the garlic cloves and lemon slice inside the chicken. Sprinkle the chicken with the thyme and marjoram.
3. Put the chicken in the air fryer basket. Surround with the potatoes and drizzle the potatoes with the remaining olive oil mixture.
4. Roast for 25 minutes, then test the temperature of the chicken. It should be 160°F. Test at the thickest part of the breast, making sure the probe doesn't touch bone. If the chicken isn't done yet, return it to the air fryer and roast it for 4 to 5 minutes, or until the temperature is 160°F. »

380°F ROAST

FAMILY FAVORITE, GLUTEN-FREE

1 (2½- to 3-pound) broiler-fryer whole chicken

2 tablespoons olive oil

½ teaspoon garlic salt

8 cloves garlic, peeled

1 slice lemon

½ teaspoon dried thyme

½ teaspoon dried marjoram

12 to 16 creamer potatoes, scrubbed

5. When the chicken is done, transfer it and the potatoes to a serving platter and cover with foil. Let the chicken rest for 5 minutes before serving.

Ingredient tip: *Creamer potatoes are small, round, white potatoes with thin and tender skins. They are usually not peeled before cooking. You can sometimes find them in boxes intended for microwave cooking in the produce department of the grocery store.*

Per serving: Calories: 491; Total Fat: 14g; Saturated Fat: 3g; Cholesterol: 175mg; Sodium: 151mg; Carbohydrates: 20g; Fiber: 3g; Protein: 68g

Chicken Cordon Bleu

PREP TIME: 15 MINUTES / COOK TIME: 13 TO 15 MINUTES / SERVES 4

Cordon bleu is French for "blue ribbon," and is the name of the famous cooking school in Paris. Chicken Cordon Bleu is chicken stuffed with ham and Swiss or Gruyère cheese. It's a fancy recipe that's a cinch to make with the air fryer.

1. Put the chicken breast filets on a work surface and gently press them with the palm of your hand to make them a bit thinner. Don't tear the meat.
2. In a small bowl, combine the ham and cheese. Divide this mixture among the chicken filets. Wrap the chicken around the filling to enclose it, using toothpicks to hold the chicken together.
3. In a shallow bowl, mix the flour, salt, pepper, and marjoram. In another bowl, beat the egg. Spread the bread crumbs out on a plate.
4. Dip the chicken into the flour mixture, then into the egg, then into the bread crumbs to coat thoroughly.
5. Put the chicken in the air fryer basket and mist with olive oil.
6. Bake for 13 to 15 minutes or until the chicken is thoroughly cooked to 165°F. Carefully remove the toothpicks and serve.

....

Ingredient tip: *You can find chicken filets, which are cut from the chicken breast, in most large grocery stores. If you can't find them, you can cut one chicken breast in half, holding your knife parallel to the work surface, to make two thin slices.*

....

Per serving: Calories: 478; Total Fat: 12g; Saturated Fat: 3g; Cholesterol: 200mg; Sodium: 575mg; Carbohydrates: 26g; Fiber: 2g; Protein: 64g

380°F FRY

FAMILY FAVORITE

4 chicken breast filets
¼ cup chopped ham
⅓ cup grated Swiss or Gruyère cheese
¼ cup flour
Pinch salt
Freshly ground black pepper
½ teaspoon dried marjoram
1 egg
1 cup panko bread crumbs
Olive oil for misting

Ham and Cheese Stuffed Chicken Burgers

PREP TIME: 12 MINUTES / COOK TIME: 13 TO 16 MINUTES / SERVES 4

Another take on the classic Chicken Cordon Bleu recipe, this dish is much more casual. Serve these tender and juicy burgers on toasted onion buns slathered with mayo and mustard and piled high with lettuce and sliced tomatoes.

350°F GRILL

FAMILY FAVORITE

⅓ cup soft bread crumbs

3 tablespoons milk

1 egg, beaten

½ teaspoon dried thyme

Pinch salt

Freshly ground black pepper

1¼ pounds ground chicken

¼ cup finely chopped ham

⅓ cup grated Havarti cheese

Olive oil for misting

1. In a medium bowl, combine the bread crumbs, milk, egg, thyme, salt, and pepper. Add the chicken and mix gently but thoroughly with clean hands.
2. Form the chicken into eight thin patties and place on waxed paper.
3. Top four of the patties with the ham and cheese. Top with remaining four patties and gently press the edges together to seal, so the ham and cheese mixture is in the middle of the burger.
4. Place the burgers in the basket and mist with olive oil. Grill for 13 to 16 minutes or until the chicken is thoroughly cooked to 165°F as measured with a meat thermometer.

Ingredient tip: *You can buy pre-chopped ham in the meat section of many supermarkets. But for this recipe, the ham should be in pieces no larger than ¼ inch. If the ham you buy is larger than that, chop it finer.*

Per serving: Calories: 367; Total Fat: 15g; Saturated Fat: 5g; Cholesterol: 179mg; Sodium: 370mg; Carbohydrates: 8g; Fiber: <1g; Protein: 47g

Chicken Tenders with Veggies

PREP TIME: 10 MINUTES / COOK TIME: 18 TO 20 MINUTES / SERVES 4

Chicken tenders cook to perfection in the air fryer. In this recipe, you'll coat them in honey and seasoned bread crumbs. Serve this homey recipe with a green salad and some garlic bread for dinner on a weeknight. Kids love it!

380°F ROAST

FAMILY FAVORITE

1 pound chicken tenders
1 tablespoon honey
Pinch salt
Freshly ground black pepper
½ cup soft fresh bread crumbs
½ teaspoon dried thyme
1 tablespoon olive oil
2 carrots, sliced
12 small red potatoes

1. In a medium bowl, toss the chicken tenders with the honey, salt, and pepper.
2. In a shallow bowl, combine the bread crumbs, thyme, and olive oil, and mix.
3. Coat the tenders in the bread crumbs, pressing firmly onto the meat.
4. Place the carrots and potatoes in the air fryer basket and top with the chicken tenders.
5. Roast for 18 to 20 minutes or until the chicken is cooked to 165°F and the vegetables are tender, shaking the basket halfway during the cooking time.

Did You Know? *Chicken tenders are cut from the chicken breast when this cut is sold boneless and skinless. The tender is a little muscle behind the breast.*

Per serving: Calories: 378; Total Fat: 8g; Saturated Fat: <1g; Cholesterol: 97mg; Sodium: 296mg; Carbohydrates: 35g; Fiber: 3g; Protein: 41g

7

MEAT

Spicy Thai Beef Stir-Fry

PREP TIME: 15 MINUTES / COOK TIME: 6 TO 9 MINUTES / SERVES 4

**370°F
STIR-FRY**

GLUTEN-FREE

1 pound sirloin
steaks, thinly
sliced

2 tablespoons
lime juice,
divided

⅓ cup crunchy
peanut butter

½ cup beef
broth

1 tablespoon
olive oil

1½ cups broccoli
florets

2 cloves garlic,
sliced

1 to 2 red chile
peppers,
sliced

Peanut butter, red chiles, and lime juice give this recipe its distinctive Thai flavor. The tender beef and broccoli, along with garlic, transform this dish into a feast.

1. In a medium bowl, combine the steak with 1 tablespoon of the lime juice. Set aside.
2. Combine the peanut butter and beef broth in a small bowl and mix well. Drain the beef and add the juice from the bowl into the peanut butter mixture.
3. In a 6-inch metal bowl, combine the olive oil, steak, and broccoli. Cook for 3 to 4 minutes or until the steak is almost cooked and the broccoli is crisp and tender, shaking the basket once during cooking time.
4. Add the garlic, chile peppers, and the peanut butter mixture and stir. Cook for 3 to 5 minutes or until the sauce is bubbling and the broccoli is tender. Serve over hot rice.

....

Did You Know? *The heat in a chile pepper is in its membranes and seeds. If you like spicy food, leave them in, but if you prefer a little less heat, remove and discard them. And when you handle chile peppers, be careful! Never touch your eyes or mouth when cutting them, because the chemical capsaicin in the peppers can burn.*

....

Per serving: Calories: 387; Total Fat: 22g; Saturated Fat: 6g; Cholesterol: 101mg; Sodium: 281mg; Carbohydrates: 7g; Fiber: 2g; Protein: 42g

Thai Burgers

PREP TIME: 10 MINUTES / COOK TIME: 15 MINUTES / SERVES 4

Did you know that ground beef, and, in fact, any ground meat, must be cooked to 165°F for food safety reasons? If the temperature is any lower, you run the risk of food poisoning. But adding a mixture of bread crumbs and liquid to the meat means you can cook that burger well done and it will still be moist and juicy.

380°F GRILL

FAMILY FAVORITE

½ cup soft bread crumbs

¼ cup Thai chili sauce

2 minced green onions

2 cloves garlic, minced

1¼ pounds 93 percent lean ground beef

4 onion rolls, split in half

1 large beefsteak tomato, sliced

⅓ cup commercial peanut sauce

1. In a large bowl, combine the bread crumbs, Thai chili sauce, green onions, and garlic, and mix well. Add the ground beef and mix gently but thoroughly until combined.
2. Form the beef mixture into four patties. Make an indentation in the center of each patty with your thumb so the burgers don't puff up when they cook.
3. Cook for 12 minutes, and then test the burgers. If they aren't at least 165°F, cook for 3 minutes until they reach that temperature.
4. Assemble burgers with the onion rolls, sliced tomato, and peanut sauce.

....

Substitution tip: *You can make these burgers with ground pork or a combination of ground pork and ground beef. You could also add sliced onions and lettuce to the burgers when you assemble them.*

....

Per serving: Calories: 584; Total Fat: 18g; Saturated Fat: 5g; Cholesterol: 127mg; Sodium: 1,315mg; Carbohydrates: 47g; Fiber: 3g; Protein: 53g

Beef Korma

PREP TIME: 10 MINUTES / COOK TIME: 17 TO 20 MINUTES / SERVES 4

350°F BAKE

GLUTEN-FREE

1 pound sirloin
    steak, sliced
½ cup yogurt
1 tablespoon
    curry powder
1 tablespoon
    olive oil
1 onion,
    chopped
2 cloves garlic,
    minced
1 tomato, diced
½ cup frozen
    baby peas,
    thawed

An Indian recipe made of a mixture of meat and vegetables, beef korma is cooked in a yogurt sauce seasoned generously with curry powder. It can be mild or spicy depending on your taste. Serve this dish with warm pita bread and a cool cucumber salad.

1. In a medium bowl, combine the steak, yogurt, and curry powder. Stir and set aside.
2. In a 6-inch metal bowl, combine the olive oil, onion, and garlic. Cook for 3 to 4 minutes or until crisp and tender.
3. Add the steak along with the yogurt and the diced tomato. Cook for 12 to 13 minutes or until steak is almost tender.
4. Stir in the peas and cook for 2 to 3 minutes or until hot.

....

Ingredient tip: *The best cuts for this recipe include sirloin, sirloin tip, and top round. The yogurt helps tenderize the steak, even with a very short marinating time.*

....

Per serving: Calories: 298; Total Fat: 11g; Saturated Fat: 4g; Cholesterol: 103mg; Sodium: 100mg; Carbohydrates: 9g; Fiber: 2g; Protein: 38g

Rice and Meatball Stuffed Bell Peppers

PREP TIME: 13 MINUTES / COOK TIME: 11 TO 17 MINUTES / SERVES 4

400°F
BAKE

FAMILY FAVORITE, GLUTEN-FREE

Stuffed peppers are classic comfort food. You can choose any color of pepper. Mix and match and let your family decide what pepper they want! Choose the tiny appetizer-size meatballs for this dish. The amount you'll need depends on the size of the peppers.

1. To prepare the peppers, cut off about ½ inch of the tops. Carefully remove the membranes and seeds from inside the peppers. Set aside.
2. In a 6-by-6-by-2-inch pan, combine the olive oil, onion, and garlic. Bake in the air fryer for 2 to 4 minutes or until crisp and tender. Remove the vegetable mixture from the pan and set aside in a medium bowl.
3. Add the rice, meatballs, tomato sauce, and mustard to the vegetable mixture and stir to combine.
4. Stuff the peppers with the meat-vegetable mixture.
5. Place the peppers in the air fryer basket and bake for 9 to 13 minutes or until the filling is hot and the peppers are tender.

....

Ingredient tip: *If you can't find small meatballs that will easily fit into the bell peppers, just buy regular-size meatballs and cut them into thirds.*

....

Per serving: Calories: 487; Total Fat: 21g; Saturated Fat: 7g; Cholesterol: 47mg; Sodium: 797mg; Carbohydrates: 57g; Fiber: 6g; Protein: 26g

4 bell peppers
1 tablespoon olive oil
1 small onion, chopped
2 cloves garlic, minced
1 cup frozen cooked rice, thawed
16 to 20 small frozen precooked meatballs, thawed
½ cup tomato sauce
2 tablespoons Dijon mustard

Stir-Fried Steak and Cabbage

PREP TIME: 10 MINUTES / COOK TIME: 8 TO 13 MINUTES / SERVES 4

**370°F
STIR-FRY**

FAMILY FAVORITE

½ pound sirloin
    steak, cut into
    strips

2 teaspoons
    cornstarch

1 tablespoon
    peanut oil

2 cups chopped
    red or green
    cabbage

1 yellow bell
    pepper,
    chopped

2 green onions,
    chopped

2 cloves garlic,
    sliced

½ cup
    commercial
    stir-fry sauce

Cabbage adds great flavor and nutrition to this simple, satisfying dish. You can use red or green cabbage—or a combination of both—in this recipe.

1. Toss the steak with the cornstarch and set aside.
2. In a 6-inch metal bowl, combine the peanut oil with the cabbage. Place in the basket and cook for 3 to 4 minutes.
3. Remove the bowl from the basket and add the steak, pepper, onions, and garlic. Return to the air fryer and cook for 3 to 5 minutes or until the steak is cooked to desired doneness and vegetables are crisp and tender.
4. Add the stir-fry sauce and cook for 2 to 4 minutes or until hot. Serve over rice.

....

Substitution tip: *In place of regular cabbage, try using Napa cabbage, which is a more traditional stir-fry ingredient. Or you could use bok choy or try broccoli florets.*

....

Per serving: Calories: 180; Total Fat: 7g; Saturated Fat: 2g; Cholesterol: 51mg; Sodium: 1,843mg; Carbohydrates: 9g; Fiber: 2g; Protein: 20g

Unstuffed Cabbage

PREP TIME: 10 MINUTES / COOK TIME: 14 TO 20 MINUTES / SERVES 4

Making traditional stuffed cabbage entails quite a bit of work. You have to soften the leaves, make the filling, stuff the cabbage, roll it up, and bake it in sauce. This one-dish version of the recipe gives you the taste of the real thing—but with much less prep work.

1. In a 6-inch metal bowl, combine the oil and the onion. Bake for 2 to 4 minutes or until the onion is crisp and tender.
2. Add the cabbage, meatballs, rice, tomatoes, marjoram, salt, and pepper, and stir.
3. Bake for 12 to 16 minutes, stirring once during cooking time, until the meatballs are hot, the rice is warmed, and the vegetables are tender.

....

Cooking tip: *At most supermarkets, you can now buy prepped fresh veggies that are ready to cook. Look in the produce section and you'll likely find chopped onions, chopped cabbage for slaw, and other foods such as shredded carrots and chopped bell peppers.*

....

Per serving: Calories: 453; Total Fat: 20g; Saturated Fat: 7g; Cholesterol: 47mg; Sodium: 590mg; Carbohydrates: 51g; Fiber: 4g; Protein: 25g

370°F BAKE

FAMILY FAVORITE, GLUTEN-FREE

1 tablespoon olive oil
1 small onion, chopped
1½ cups chopped green cabbage
16 precooked frozen meatballs
1 cup frozen cooked rice
2 tomatoes, chopped
½ teaspoon dried marjoram
Pinch salt
Freshly ground black pepper

Cheese-Stuffed Meatballs

PREP TIME: 15 MINUTES / COOK TIME: 10 TO 13 MINUTES / SERVES 4

**390°F
BAKE**

FAMILY FAVORITE

⅓ cup soft bread crumbs

3 tablespoons milk

1 tablespoon ketchup

1 egg

½ teaspoon dried marjoram

Pinch salt

Freshly ground black pepper

1 pound 95 percent lean ground beef

20 ½-inch cubes of cheese

Olive oil for misting

Meatballs that are stuffed with melted cheese are divine! They are easy to make, albeit a bit fussy. In this recipe, feel free to use any kind of cheese that melts easily, from mozzarella to Swiss or Colby. Serve them with pasta sauce over noodles or rice.

1. In a large bowl, combine the bread crumbs, milk, ketchup, egg, marjoram, salt, and pepper, and mix well.
2. Add the ground beef and mix gently but thoroughly with your hands.
3. Form the mixture into 20 meatballs.
4. Shape each meatball around a cheese cube. Mist the meatballs with olive oil and put into the air fryer basket.
5. Bake for 10 to 13 minutes or until the meatballs register 165°F on a meat thermometer.

....

Cooking tip: *To make the best meatballs or meatloaf, always combine all of the "filler" ingredients—such as bread crumbs and egg—first, then mix in the meat. The more you handle the meat, the tougher the meatballs. Handle ground meat as little as possible for best results.*

....

Per serving: Calories: 393; Total Fat: 17g; Saturated Fat: 8g; Cholesterol: 166mg; Sodium: 499mg; Carbohydrates: 10g; Fiber: 0g; Protein: 50g

Meatballs in Spicy Tomato Sauce

PREP TIME: 10 MINUTES / COOK TIME: 11 TO 15 MINUTES / SERVES 4

Meatballs may become your air fryer go-to: You can make moist meatballs with a slightly crisp crust with much less effort than you'd expend making them on the stovetop. To avoid smoke, use ground beef that is at least 95 percent lean.

1. In a large bowl, combine the green onions, garlic, egg yolk, cracker crumbs, salt, and pepper, and mix well.
2. Add the ground beef and mix gently but thoroughly with your hands until combined. Form into 1½-inch meatballs.
3. Mist the meatballs with olive oil and put into the basket of the air fryer.
4. Bake for 8 to 11 minutes or until the meatballs are 165°F.
5. Remove the meatballs from the basket and place in a 6-inch metal bowl. Top with the pasta sauce and Dijon mustard and mix gently.
6. Bake for 3 to 4 minutes or until the sauce is hot.

....

Substitution tip: *You can make these meatballs with lean ground pork, or ground chicken or turkey, or a combination of any of those meats. Just make sure you cook them until they register an internal temperature of 165°F for food safety reasons.*

....

Per serving: Calories: 360; Total Fat: 12g; Saturated Fat: 4g; Cholesterol: 154mg; Sodium: 875mg; Carbohydrates: 24g; Fiber: 3g; Protein: 39g

400°F BAKE

FAMILY FAVORITE

3 green onions, minced
1 garlic clove, minced
1 egg yolk
¼ cup saltine cracker crumbs
Pinch salt
Freshly ground black pepper
1 pound 95 percent lean ground beef
Olive oil for misting
1¼ cups pasta sauce (from a 16-ounce jar)
2 tablespoons Dijon mustard

Mexican Pizza

PREP TIME: 10 MINUTES / COOK TIME: 7 TO 9 MINUTES / SERVES 4

**370°F
BAKE**

FAMILY FAVORITE

¾ cup refried
  beans (from a
  16-ounce can)
½ cup salsa
10 frozen
  precooked
  beef meat-
  balls, thawed
  and sliced
1 jalapeño
  pepper, sliced
4 whole-wheat
  pita breads
1 cup shredded
  pepper Jack
  cheese
½ cup shredded
  Colby cheese
⅓ cup sour
  cream

You may be surprised to learn that pizza bakes beautifully—and quickly—in the air fryer! The crust crisps up, the cheese melts to perfection, and the toppings get hot and remain firm, not soggy. This recipe provides a spicy twist to a classic pie.

1. In a medium bowl, combine the refried beans, salsa, meatballs, and jalapeño pepper.
2. Preheat the air fryer for 3 to 4 minutes or until hot.
3. Top the pitas with the refried bean mixture and sprinkle with the cheeses.
4. Bake for 7 to 9 minutes or until the pizza is crisp and the cheese is melted and starts to brown.
5. Top each pizza with a dollop of sour cream and serve warm.

....

Substitution tip: *If you like, add cooked pork sausage to this recipe. Or add other vegetables, such as mushrooms, chopped onion, or chopped tomatoes to the refried bean mixture.*

....

Per serving: Calories: 510; Total Fat: 24g; Saturated Fat: 12g; Cholesterol: 64mg; Sodium: 1,196mg; Carbohydrates: 50g; Fiber: 9g; Protein: 31g

Tex-Mex Steak

PREP TIME: 25 MINUTES / COOK TIME: 20 MINUTES / SERVES 4

Who needs a grill when you have an air fryer? This recipe takes longer than 30 minutes from start to finish, but it's worth the wait. It features the classic spicy flavors of Mexican dishes; the steak gets its kick from chipotle peppers and red pepper flakes.

390°F GRILL

GLUTEN-FREE

1 pound skirt steak

1 chipotle pepper in adobo sauce, minced (La Costena or another gluten-free brand)

2 tablespoons adobo sauce (La Costena or another gluten-free brand)

½ teaspoon salt

⅛ teaspoon pepper

⅛ teaspoon crushed red pepper flakes

1. Cut the steak into four pieces and place them on a plate.
2. In a small bowl, combine the minced chipotle pepper, adobo sauce, salt, pepper, and crushed red pepper flakes. Spread over the steaks on both sides.
3. Let the steaks stand at room temperature for at least 20 minutes, or refrigerate up to 12 hours.
4. Grill the steaks, two at a time, in the air fryer basket for 10 minutes until the steaks register an internal temperature of at least 145°F. Repeat with remaining steaks while the first ones rest, covered with foil.
5. Add the just-cooked steaks to the ones that have been resting and let rest for another 5 minutes. Slice thinly across the grain to serve.

....

Ingredient tip: *Chipotles in adobo are jalapeño peppers that are cooked and jarred in a spicy red sauce. Many adobo sauces contain gluten, so read the labels carefully or opt for gluten-free La Costena brand.*

....

Per serving: Calories: 244; Total Fat: 11g; Saturated Fat: 4g; Cholesterol: 67mg; Sodium: 617mg; Carbohydrates: 3g; Fiber: 0g; Protein: 30g

Chicken-Fried Steak

PREP TIME: 15 MINUTES / COOK TIME: 15 MINUTES / SERVES 4

**350°F
FRY**

FAMILY FAVORITE

4 (6-ounce) beef
  cube steaks
½ cup buttermilk
1 cup flour
2 teaspoons
  paprika
1 teaspoon
  garlic salt
1 egg
1 cup soft bread
  crumbs
2 tablespoons
  olive oil

"Chicken-fried" steak doesn't contain any chicken! It's simply a method for cooking steak that is similar to fried chicken. The steak is coated in a batter and deep-fried until crisp on the outside and juicy on the inside. For the air fryer, a batter alone wouldn't create the desired crust, so here you add bread crumbs to the mix.

1. Place the cube steaks on a plate or cutting board and gently pound until they are slightly thinner. Set aside.
2. In a shallow bowl, combine the buttermilk, flour, paprika, garlic salt, and egg until just combined.
3. On a plate, combine the bread crumbs and olive oil and mix well.
4. Dip the steaks into the buttermilk batter to coat, and let sit on a plate for 5 minutes.
5. Dredge the steaks in the bread crumbs. Pat the crumbs onto both sides to coat the steaks thoroughly.
6. Air-fry the steaks for 12 to 16 minutes or until the meat reaches 160°F on a meat thermometer and the coating is brown and crisp. You can serve this with heated beef gravy.

....

Did You Know? *Cube steaks have been "mechanically tenderized" and have to be cooked to well done. The meat has been pierced with needles or blades to cut up the fibers in the meat so it will be tender when cooked. This also means that bacteria on the surface of the meat have been pushed through to the inside. For safety reasons, cook this type of steak to 160°F.*

....

Per serving: Calories: 630; Total Fat: 21g; Saturated Fat: 6g; Cholesterol: 194mg; Sodium: 358mg; Carbohydrates: 46g; Fiber: 3g; Protein: 61g

Tender Country Ribs

PREP TIME: 5 MINUTES / COOK TIME: 20 TO 25 MINUTES / SERVES 4

Country-style pork ribs are much meatier than spareribs. You can buy them with or without the bone. For this recipe, opt for bone-less ribs. When cooked in the air fryer, you get the depth of flavor of traditional ribs in a fraction of the time.

1. Place the ribs on a clean work surface.
2. In a small bowl, combine the cornstarch, olive oil, mustard, thyme, garlic powder, marjoram, salt, and pepper, and rub into the ribs.
3. Place the ribs in the air fryer basket and roast for 10 minutes.
4. Carefully turn the ribs using tongs and roast for 10 to 15 minutes or until the ribs are crisp and register an internal temperature of at least 150°F.

....

Air Fryer tip: *When you turn the ribs, you may want to remove excess grease from the air fryer pan that sits below the basket. Put the pan and basket on a heatproof surface and carefully push the button to release the basket. Drain the fat from the pan and put the basket back on it. Reattach and continue cooking.*

....

Per serving: Calories: 578; Total Fat: 44g; Saturated Fat: 14g; Cholesterol: 1153mg; Sodium: 155mg; Carbohydrates: 4g; Fiber: 0g; Protein: 40g

400°F ROAST

FAMILY FAVORITE, GLUTEN-FREE

12 country-style pork ribs, trimmed of excess fat

2 tablespoons cornstarch

2 tablespoons olive oil

1 teaspoon dry mustard

½ teaspoon thyme

½ teaspoon garlic powder

1 teaspoon dried marjoram

Pinch salt

Freshly ground black pepper

Bacon Garlic Pizza

PREP TIME: 10 MINUTES / COOK TIME: 20 MINUTES / SERVES 4

370°F
BAKE

FAMILY FAVORITE

Flour, for
dusting
4 frozen large
whole-wheat
dinner rolls,
thawed
Nonstick baking
spray with
flour
5 cloves garlic,
minced
¾ cup pizza
sauce
½ teaspoon
dried oregano
½ teaspoon
garlic salt
8 slices
precooked
bacon, cut
into 1-inch
pieces
1¼ cups
shredded
Cheddar
cheese

Frozen dinner rolls make great crusts for individual pizzas. This dough is stiffer than most pizza dough in a tube and forms a crispier crust. Shaping the pizza into an oval means you can bake two at a time, which gets dinner on the table more quickly.

1. On a lightly floured surface, press out each dinner roll to a 5-by-3-inch oval.
2. Spray four 6-by-4-inch pieces of heavy duty foil with nonstick spray and place one crust on each piece.
3. Bake, two at a time, for 2 minutes or until the crusts are set, but not browned.
4. Meanwhile, in a small bowl, combine the garlic, pizza sauce, oregano, and garlic salt. When the pizza crusts are set, spread each with some of the sauce. Top with the bacon pieces and Cheddar cheese.
5. Bake, two at a time, for another 8 minutes or until the crust is browned and the cheese is melted and starting to brown.

....

Substitution tip: *You can use this recipe as a basis for just about any pizza you'd like. Use pepperoni instead of the bacon. Use Swiss or mozzarella cheese in place of the Cheddar. And add any vegetable, such as sliced mushrooms or chopped green onions, that you like.*

....

Per serving: Calories: 739; Total Fat: 42g; Saturated Fat: 19g; Cholesterol: 102mg; Sodium: 1,685mg; Carbohydrates: 53g; Fiber: 3g; Protein: 37g

Sweet-and-Sour Polish Sausage

PREP TIME: 10 MINUTES / COOK TIME: 10 TO 15 MINUTES / SERVES 4

Polish sausage cooks very well in the air fryer. The skin gets crisp and the inside stays moist and juicy, even when it is cut into pieces before cooking. When cooked in a sweet-and-sour sauce with some vegetables, this sausage becomes a hearty dinner dish. Enjoy over rice.

1. Cut the sausage into 1½-inch pieces and put into a 6-inch metal bowl. Add the pepper and minced onion.
2. In a small bowl, combine the brown sugar, ketchup, mustard, apple cider vinegar, and chicken broth, and mix well. Pour into the bowl.
3. Roast for 10 to 15 minutes or until the sausage is hot, the vegetables tender, and the sauce bubbling and slightly thickened.

....

Did You Know? *Polish sausage is almost always fully cooked when it is sold; read the label carefully to make sure you buy a fully cooked type for this recipe. Uncooked sausages are too fatty and release too much grease to cook in this appliance.*

....

Per serving: Calories: 381; Total Fat: 26g; Saturated Fat: 8g; Cholesterol: 71mg; Sodium: 957mg; Carbohydrates: 17g; Fiber: 2g; Protein: 19g

350°F ROAST

FAMILY FAVORITE

¾ pound Polish sausage

1 red bell pepper, cut into 1-inch strips

½ cup minced onion

3 tablespoons brown sugar

⅓ cup ketchup

2 tablespoons mustard

2 tablespoons apple cider vinegar

½ cup chicken broth

Lemon Pork Tenderloin

PREP TIME: 5 MINUTES / COOK TIME: 10 MINUTES / SERVES 4

**400°F
ROAST**
—

**FAST, FAMILY
FAVORITE,
GLUTEN-FREE**

1 (1-pound)
    pork tender-
    loin, cut into
    ½-inch slices
1 tablespoon
    olive oil
1 tablespoon
    lemon juice
1 tablespoon
    honey
½ teaspoon
    grated lemon
    zest
½ teaspoon
    dried
    marjoram
Pinch salt
Freshly ground
    black pepper

Because it comes from a part on the animal near the rib cage that is rarely used, pork tenderloin is one of the most tender cuts of meat. It absorbs flavors readily and cooks quickly, which lets you put dinner on the table in mere minutes.

1. Put the pork tenderloin slices in a medium bowl.
2. In a small bowl, combine the olive oil, lemon juice, honey, lemon zest, marjoram, salt, and pepper. Mix together.
3. Pour this marinade over the tenderloin slices and massage gently with your hand to work it into the pork.
4. Place the pork in the air fryer basket and roast for 10 minutes or until the pork registers at least 145°F using a meat thermometer.

....

Ingredient tip: *You can often buy pre-marinated pork tenderloin in the supermarket, which makes this meat even faster to prepare. Just slice the pork and cook and you could eat in 10 minutes!*

....

Per serving: Calories: 209; Total Fat: 8g; Saturated Fat: 2g; Cholesterol: 83mg; Sodium: 104mg; Carbohydrates: 5g; Fiber: 0g; Protein: 30g

Crispy Mustard Pork Tenderloin

PREP TIME: 10 MINUTES / COOK TIME: 13 MINUTES / SERVES 4

Pork tenderloin is the most tender cut of the pig. When coated with mustard and minced garlic, then bread crumbs, this meat crisps up on the outside and remains juicy on the inside. Serve with roasted potatoes and a fruit salad for a satisfying dinner.

1. Slightly pound the pork slices until they are about ¾-inch thick. Sprinkle with salt and pepper on both sides.
2. Coat the pork with the mustard and sprinkle with the garlic and basil.
3. On a plate, combine the bread crumbs and olive oil and mix well. Coat the pork slices with the bread crumb mixture, patting so the crumbs adhere.
4. Place the pork in the air fryer basket, leaving a little space between each piece. Air-fry for 12 to 14 minutes or until the pork reaches at least 145°F on a meat thermometer and the coating is crisp and brown. Serve immediately.

....

Ingredient tip: *When you buy pork tenderloin at the grocery store, be sure to read the label. This cut is often sold marinated, and you don't want the flavors in the marinade to clash with the flavors in this recipe. For this recipe, look for plain tenderloin that is not marinated.*

....

Per serving: Calories: 335; Total Fat: 13g; Saturated Fat: 3g; Cholesterol: 83mg; Sodium: 390mg; Carbohydrates: 20g; Fiber: 2g; Protein: 34g

390°F FRY

FAMILY FAVORITE

1 pound pork tenderloin, cut into 1-inch slices

Pinch salt

Freshly ground black pepper

2 tablespoons Dijon mustard

1 clove garlic, minced

½ teaspoon dried basil

1 cup soft bread crumbs

2 tablespoons olive oil

8

VEGETABLES AND SIDES

Roasted Potato Salad

PREP TIME: 5 MINUTES / COOK TIME: 25 MINUTES / SERVES 4 TO 6

Potato salad is a versatile dish to serve any time of the year. This salad is served warm, but you can cool it for serving later. The hot potatoes will soak up the lemony dressing.

350°F
ROAST

FAMILY FAVORITE, VEGETARIAN, GLUTEN-FREE

2 pounds tiny red or creamer potatoes, cut in half

1 tablespoon plus ⅓ cup olive oil

Pinch salt

Freshly ground black pepper

1 red bell pepper, chopped

2 green onions, chopped

⅓ cup lemon juice

3 tablespoons Dijon or yellow mustard

1. Place the potatoes in the air fryer basket and drizzle with 1 tablespoon of the olive oil. Sprinkle with salt and pepper.
2. Roast for 25 minutes, shaking twice during cooking time, until the potatoes are tender and light golden brown.
3. Meanwhile, place the bell pepper and green onions in a large bowl.
4. In a small bowl, combine the remaining ⅓ cup of olive oil, the lemon juice, and mustard, and mix well with a whisk.
5. When the potatoes are cooked, add them to the bowl with the bell peppers and top with the dressing. Toss gently to coat.
6. Let cool for 20 minutes. Stir gently again and serve or refrigerate and serve later.

Variation tip: *You can brighten and add complexity to this dish by adding lots of fresh chopped herbs. Try chopped dill, basil, or rosemary, depending on your preference. The warmth of the potatoes will deepen the herbs' flavor.*

Per serving: Calories: 353; Total Fat: 21g; Saturated Fat: 3g; Cholesterol: 0mg; Sodium: 192mg; Carbohydrates: 39g; Fiber: 7g; Protein: 5g

Creamy Corn Casserole

PREP TIME: 5 MINUTES / COOK TIME: 15 MINUTES / SERVES 4

A corn casserole is comforting and homey, and the perfect side dish for meatloaf or a roast chicken. This classic recipe whips up quickly when cooked in the air fryer.

1. Spray a 6-by-6-by-2-inch baking pan with nonstick spray.
2. In a medium bowl, combine the corn, flour, egg, milk, and light cream, and mix until combined. Stir in the cheese, salt, and pepper.
3. Pour this mixture into the prepared baking pan. Dot with the butter.
4. Bake for 15 minutes.

....

Substitution tip: *You can substitute one 15-ounce can of corn, drained, for the frozen corn. Or cut the kernels off 2 to 3 ears of corn to use in this recipe.*

....

Per serving: Calories: 255; Total Fat: 16g; Saturated Fat: 10g; Cholesterol: 87mg; Sodium: 136mg; Carbohydrates: 21g; Fiber: 2g; Protein: 9g

320°F BAKE

FAMILY FAVORITE, VEGETARIAN

Nonstick baking spray with flour
2 cups frozen yellow corn
3 tablespoons flour
1 egg, beaten
¼ cup milk
½ cup light cream
½ cup grated Swiss or Havarti cheese
Pinch salt
Freshly ground black pepper
2 tablespoons butter, cut in cubes

9

DESSERTS

Grilled Curried Fruit

PREP TIME: 10 MINUTES / COOK TIME: 7 MINUTES / SERVES 6 TO 8

**350°F
GRILL**

**FAST,
VEGETARIAN,
GLUTEN-FREE**

2 peaches
2 firm pears
2 plums
2 tablespoons
   melted butter
1 tablespoon
   honey
2 to 3 teaspoons
   curry powder

If you've never had grilled fruit before, here's a wonderful introduction. Grilling caramelizes the sugars in fruits, brings out their flavor, and even turns fruit that's not quite ripe into a sweet dessert. Serve with some sherbet or ice cream for a cooling contrast.

1. Cut the peaches in half, remove the pits, and cut each half in half again. Cut the pears in half, core them, and remove the stem. Cut each half in half again. Do the same with the plums.
2. Spread a large sheet of heavy-duty foil on your work surface. Arrange the fruit on the foil and drizzle with the butter and honey. Sprinkle with the curry powder.
3. Wrap the fruit in the foil, making sure to leave some air space in the packet.
4. Put the foil package in the basket and grill for 5 to 8 minutes, shaking the basket once during the cooking time, until the fruit is soft and tender.

....

Ingredient tip: *Cut pears oxidize quickly, resulting in brown fruit. You can prevent browning by squeezing a little bit of fresh lemon juice onto the slices. The ascorbic acid in the lemon works to combat oxidation.*

....

Per serving: Calories: 107; Total Fat: 4g; Saturated Fat: 3g; Cholesterol: 10mg; Sodium: 29mg; Carbohydrates: 19g; Fiber: 3g; Protein: <1g

Apple Peach Cranberry Crisp

PREP TIME: 10 MINUTES / COOK TIME: 11 MINUTES / SERVES 8

A crisp is a combination of cooked fruit topped with a sweet streusel. This classic dessert is perfect for fall dinners. Serve with a scoop of ice cream or softly whipped cream flavored with vanilla.

1. In a 6-by-6-by-2-inch pan, combine the apple, peaches, cranberries, and honey, and mix well.
2. In a medium bowl, combine the brown sugar, flour, oatmeal, and butter, and mix until crumbly. Sprinkle this mixture over the fruit in the pan.
3. Bake for 10 to 12 minutes or until the fruit is bubbly and the topping is golden brown. Serve warm.

....

Substitution tip: *Other fruits can be used in this recipe. Try chopped plums or nectarines instead of the apple and peaches. Or use golden raisins or currants in place of the dried cranberries.*

....

Per serving: Calories: 134; Total Fat: 5g; Saturated Fat: 3g; Cholesterol: 11mg; Sodium: 33mg; Carbohydrates: 23g; Fiber: 2g; Protein: 1g

380°F BAKE

FAMILY FAVORITE, VEGETARIAN

1 apple, peeled and chopped
2 peaches, peeled and chopped
⅓ cup dried cranberries
2 tablespoons honey
⅓ cup brown sugar
¼ cup flour
½ cup oatmeal
3 tablespoons softened butter

Orange Cornmeal Cake

PREP TIME: 7 MINUTES / COOK TIME: 23 MINUTES / SERVES 8

340°F
BAKE

FAMILY FAVORITE,
VEGETARIAN

Nonstick baking
spray with
flour
1¼ cups all-
purpose flour
⅓ cup yellow
cornmeal
¾ cup white
sugar
1 teaspoon
baking soda
¼ cup safflower
oil
1¼ cups orange
juice, divided
1 teaspoon
vanilla
¼ cup powdered
sugar

Cornmeal adds wonderful flavor and a bit of crunch to this tender cake recipe. An orange glaze is poured over the cake when it's still hot and soaks into the crumb. Serve this cake with a cup of coffee for a breakfast treat or afternoon snack.

1. Spray a 6-by-6-by-2-inch baking pan with nonstick spray and set aside.
2. In a medium bowl, combine the flour, cornmeal, sugar, baking soda, safflower oil, 1 cup of the orange juice, and vanilla, and mix well.
3. Pour the batter into the baking pan and place in the air fryer. Bake for 23 minutes or until a toothpick inserted in the center of the cake comes out clean.
4. Remove the cake from the basket and place on a cooling rack. Using a toothpick, make about 20 holes in the cake.
5. In a small bowl, combine remaining ¼ cup of orange juice and the powdered sugar and stir well. Drizzle this mixture over the hot cake slowly so the cake absorbs it.
6. Cool completely, then cut into wedges to serve.

....

Did You Know? *To test for doneness when baking cakes, there are a few rules. A cake should spring back lightly when gently touched with a finger. Or, you can insert a clean toothpick into the cake; it should come out clean. Finally, when a cake is done, it starts to pull away from the sides of the baking pan slightly.*

....

Per serving: Calories: 253; Total Fat: 7g; Saturated Fat: <1g; Cholesterol: 45mg; Sodium: 161mg; Carbohydrates: 45g; Fiber: 1g; Protein: 3g

Black Forest Hand Pies

PREP TIME: 10 MINUTES / COOK TIME: 15 MINUTES / SERVES 6

Black Forest Torte is an old-world cake with chocolate and cherries. This easy recipe is fun to make, and kids especially love it. The chocolate and cherries are encased in puff pastry, which cooks to perfection in the air fryer. These taste delicious warm or cold.

1. In a small bowl, combine the chocolate chips, fudge sauce, and dried cherries.
2. Roll out the puff pastry on a floured surface. Cut into 6 squares with a sharp knife.
3. Divide the chocolate chip mixture onto the center of each puff pastry square. Fold the squares in half to make triangles. Firmly press the edges with the tines of a fork to seal.
4. Brush the triangles on all sides sparingly with the beaten egg white. Sprinkle the tops with sugar and cinnamon.
5. Place in the air fryer basket and bake for 15 minutes or until the triangles are golden brown. The filling will be hot, so cool for at least 20 minutes before serving.

....

Air Fryer tip: *Make sure that these little pies are not touching each other in the air fryer so they brown and crisp on all sides.*

....

Per serving: Calories: 173; Total Fat: 9g; Saturated Fat: 3g; Cholesterol: 1mg; Sodium: 62mg; Carbohydrates: 21g; Fiber: <1g; Protein: 3g

300°F BAKE

FAMILY FAVORITE, VEGETARIAN

3 tablespoons milk or dark chocolate chips

2 tablespoons thick, hot fudge sauce

2 tablespoons chopped dried cherries

1 (10-by-15-inch) sheet puff pastry, thawed

1 egg white, beaten

2 tablespoons sugar

½ teaspoon cinnamon

Marble Cheesecake

PREP TIME: 10 MINUTES / COOK TIME: 20 MINUTES / SERVES 8

**320°F
BAKE**

**FAMILY FAVORITE,
VEGETARIAN**

1 cup graham
    cracker
    crumbs
3 tablespoons
    softened
    butter
1½ (8-ounce)
    packages
    cream cheese,
    softened
⅓ cup sugar
2 eggs, beaten
1 tablespoon
    flour
1 teaspoon
    vanilla
¼ cup chocolate
    syrup

A cheesecake cooked in the air fryer seems improbable, but it works! This cheesecake is a combination of vanilla and chocolate. It's not only delicious, it's gorgeous, too. Splurge and enjoy for dessert after a weeknight meal.

1. For the crust, combine the graham cracker crumbs and butter in a small bowl and mix well. Press into the bottom of a 6-by-6-by-2-inch baking pan and put in the freezer to set.
2. For the filling, combine the cream cheese and sugar in a medium bowl and mix well. Beat in the eggs, one at a time. Add the flour and vanilla.
3. Remove ⅔ cup of the filling to a small bowl and stir in the chocolate syrup until combined.
4. Pour the vanilla filling into the pan with the crust. Drop the chocolate filling over the vanilla filling by the spoonful. With a clean butter knife stir the fillings in a zigzag pattern to marbleize them.
5. Bake for 20 minutes or until the cheesecake is just set.
6. Cool on a wire rack for 1 hour, then chill in the refrigerator until the cheesecake is firm.

....

Substitution tip: *Using this basic recipe, you can make other flavors. Add ½ cup chocolate syrup and don't divide the batter for a chocolate cheesecake. Omit the chocolate syrup and add about ⅓ cup of lemon curd for a lemon cheesecake.*

....

Per serving: Calories: 311; Total Fat: 21g; Saturated Fat: 13g; Cholesterol: 99mg; Sodium: 272mg; Carbohydrates: 25g; Fiber: 1g; Protein: 6g

Black and White Brownies

PREP TIME: 10 MINUTES / COOK TIME: 20 MINUTES /
MAKES 1 DOZEN BROWNIES

Who doesn't love brownies? In the air fryer, the brownies stay moist and deeply rich, but get the most wonderful crunchy and crisp top. This easy recipe should quickly become part of your regular air frying repertoire.

1. In a medium bowl, beat the egg with the brown sugar and white sugar. Beat in the oil and vanilla.
2. Add the cocoa powder and flour, and stir just until combined. Fold in the white chocolate chips.
3. Spray a 6-by-6-by-2-inch baking pan with nonstick spray. Spoon the brownie batter into the pan.
4. Bake for 20 minutes or until the brownies are set when lightly touched with a finger. Let cool for 30 minutes before slicing to serve.

....

Cooking tip: *You measure cocoa powder just like you measure flour: spoon it lightly into a measuring cup and level off the top with the back of a knife. Never scoop flour or dry ingredients into a measuring cup because that adds too much to the recipe and your cookies, cakes, and bars will be dense and heavy.*

....

Per serving: Calories: 81; Total Fat: 4g; Saturated Fat: 1g; Cholesterol: 14mg; Sodium: 10mg; Carbohydrates: 11g; Fiber: <1g; Protein: 1g

340°F
BAKE

FAMILY FAVORITE, VEGETARIAN

1 egg
¼ cup brown sugar
2 tablespoons white sugar
2 tablespoons safflower oil
1 teaspoon vanilla
¼ cup cocoa powder
⅓ cup all-purpose flour
¼ cup white chocolate chips
Nonstick baking spray with flour

Chocolate Peanut Butter Molten Cupcakes

PREP TIME: 15 MINUTES / COOK TIME: 10 TO 13 MINUTES / MAKES 8 CUPCAKES

320°F BAKE

FAMILY FAVORITE, VEGETARIAN

Nonstick baking spray with flour
1⅓ cups chocolate cake mix (from 15-ounce box)
1 egg
1 egg yolk
¼ cup safflower oil
¼ cup hot water
⅓ cup sour cream
3 tablespoons peanut butter
1 tablespoon powdered sugar

Molten cupcakes are cakes that are slightly underbaked so the center stays runny. This recipe is a bit different: A ball of peanut butter and powdered sugar is added to the middle of each cupcake before baking. It softens as the cake bakes, creating a molten middle of sweet peanut butter. Serve these cupcakes warm with vanilla ice cream.

1. Double up 16 foil muffin cups to make 8 cups. Spray each lightly with nonstick spray; set aside.
2. In a medium bowl, combine the cake mix, egg, egg yolk, safflower oil, water, and sour cream, and beat until combined.
3. In a small bowl, combine the peanut butter and powdered sugar and mix well. Form this mixture into 8 balls.
4. Spoon about ¼ cup of the chocolate batter into each muffin cup and top with a peanut butter ball. Spoon remaining batter on top of the peanut butter balls to cover them.
5. Arrange the cups in the air fryer basket, leaving some space between each. Bake for 10 to 13 minutes or until the tops look dry and set.
6. Let the cupcakes cool for about 10 minutes, then serve warm.

....

Ingredient tip: Save the rest of the chocolate cake mix in a sealed heavy-duty plastic bag. Be sure to mark it with the date that you used it. Use it within two weeks—maybe to make more batches of this recipe!

....

Per serving: Calories: 195; Total Fat: 15g; Saturated Fat: 3g; Cholesterol: 51mg; Sodium: 158mg; Carbohydrates: 13g; Fiber: <1g; Protein: 4g

Chocolate Peanut Butter Bread Pudding

PREP TIME: 10 MINUTES / COOK TIME: 10 TO 12 MINUTES / SERVES 8

Bread pudding is the ultimate comfort food. The addition of chocolate and peanut butter adds a subtle richness to this recipe and intensifies the flavors. Serve with heavy whipped cream to double the indulgence.

1. Spray a 6-by-6-by-2-inch baking pan with nonstick spray.
2. In a medium bowl, combine the egg, egg yolk, chocolate milk, cocoa, brown sugar, peanut butter, and vanilla, and mix until combined. Stir in the bread cubes and let soak for 10 minutes.
3. Spoon this mixture into the prepared pan. Bake for 10 to 12 minutes or until the pudding is firm to the touch.

....

Substitution tip: *Use different types of bread in this recipe. You could use cubed doughnuts, or try a quick bread such as banana bread or peanut butter bread.*

....

Per serving: Calories: 102; Total Fat: 5g; Saturated Fat: 2g; Cholesterol: 50mg; Sodium: 90mg; Carbohydrates: 11g; Fiber: 1g; Protein: 4g

330°F BAKE

FAMILY FAVORITE, VEGETARIAN

Nonstick baking spray with flour

1 egg

1 egg yolk

¾ cup chocolate milk

2 tablespoons cocoa powder

3 tablespoons brown sugar

3 tablespoons peanut butter

1 teaspoon vanilla

5 slices firm white bread, cubed

Big Chocolate Chip Cookie

PREP TIME: 10 MINUTES / COOK TIME: 9 MINUTES / SERVES 4

300°F BAKE

FAST, FAMILY FAVORITE, VEGETARIAN

3 tablespoons softened butter

⅓ cup plus 1 tablespoon brown sugar

1 egg yolk

½ cup flour

2 tablespoons ground white chocolate

¼ teaspoon baking soda

½ teaspoon vanilla

¾ cup chocolate chips

Nonstick baking spray with flour

Everyone loves chocolate chip cookies. But have you ever made one that was 6 inches in diameter? This fun recipe makes one big cookie that serves four people. Everyone breaks off a piece to enjoy. This cookie is especially wonderful served warm.

1. In medium bowl, beat the butter and brown sugar together until fluffy. Stir in the egg yolk.
2. Add the flour, white chocolate, baking soda, and vanilla, and mix well. Stir in the chocolate chips.
3. Line a 6-by-6-by-2-inch baking pan with parchment paper. Spray the parchment paper with nonstick baking spray with flour.
4. Spread the batter into the prepared pan, leaving a ½-inch border on all sides.
5. Bake for about 9 minutes or until the cookie is light brown and just barely set.
6. Remove the pan from the air fryer and let cool for 10 minutes. Remove the cookie from the pan, remove the parchment paper, and let cool on a wire rack.

....

Substitution tip: *You can use other types of chocolate chips in this recipe. Try milk chocolate chips or butterscotch chips. Or add about ¼ cup chopped pecans or cashews when you stir in the chocolate chips.*

....

Per serving: Calories: 309; Total Fat: 22g; Saturated Fat: 14g; Cholesterol: 84mg; Sodium: 178mg; Carbohydrates: 49g; Fiber: 2g; Protein: 5g

Frosted Peanut Butter Cookie

PREP TIME: 10 MINUTES / COOK TIME: 10 MINUTES / SERVES 4

A giant peanut butter cookie topped with melted chocolate is the perfect dessert on a weeknight. Eat this cookie warm while the frosting is still soft for an indulgent treat.

**310°F
BAKE**

**FAMILY FAVORITE,
VEGETARIAN**

1. In a medium bowl, beat the butter and brown sugar together until fluffy. Stir in the egg yolk.
2. Add the flour, 3 tablespoons of the peanut butter, the baking soda, and vanilla, and mix well.
3. Line a 6-by-6-by-2-inch baking pan with parchment paper.
4. Spread the batter into the prepared pan, leaving a ½-inch border on all sides.
5. Bake for 7 to 10 minutes or until the cookie is light brown and just barely set.
6. Remove the pan from the air fryer and let cool for 10 minutes. Remove the cookie from the pan, remove the parchment paper, and let cool on a wire rack.
7. In a small heatproof cup, combine the chocolate chips with the remaining 2 tablespoons of peanut butter. Bake for 1 to 2 minutes or until the chips are melted. Stir to combine and spread on the cookie.

3 tablespoons
   butter,
   at room
   temperature
⅓ cup plus
   1 tablespoon
   brown sugar
1 egg yolk
⅔ cup flour
5 tablespoons
   peanut butter,
   divided
¼ teaspoon
   baking soda
1 teaspoon
   vanilla
½ cup
   semisweet
   chocolate
   chips

....

Variation tip: *You can double or triple this recipe. You can also serve the cookie unfrosted, or combine 2 tablespoons soft butter, 2 tablespoons peanut butter, and ½ cup powdered sugar, mix well, and use to frost the cookie.*

....

Per serving: Calories: 481; Total Fat: 28g; Saturated Fat: 13g; Cholesterol: 75mg; Sodium: 239mg; Carbohydrates: 52g; Fiber: 3g; Protein: 8g

The Dirty Dozen and the Clean Fifteen

A nonprofit and environmental watchdog organization called Environmental Working Group (EWG) looks at data supplied by the U.S. Department of Agriculture (USDA) and the Food and Drug Administration (FDA) about pesticide residues and compiles a list each year of the lowest and highest pesticide loads found in commercial crops. You can refer to the Dirty Dozen list to know which fruits and vegetables you should always buy organic. The Clean Fifteen list tells you which produce is considered safe enough when grown conventionally to allow you to skip the organics. This does not mean that the Clean Fifteen produce is pesticide-free, though, so wash these fruits and vegetables thoroughly. These lists change every year, so make sure you look up the most recent list before you fill your shopping cart. You'll find the most current as well as a guide to pesticides in produce at www.EWG.org/FoodNews.

DIRTY DOZEN	CLEAN FIFTEEN
Apples	Asparagus
Celery	Avocados
Cherries	Cabbage
Cherry tomatoes	Cantaloupe
Cucumbers	Cauliflower
Grapes	Eggplant
Nectarines	Grapefruit
Peaches	Honeydew melons
Spinach	Kiwis
Strawberries	Mangos
Sweet bell peppers	Onions
Tomatoes	Papayas
	Pineapples
In addition to the Dirty Dozen, the EWG added two foods contaminated with highly toxic organo-phosphate insecticides:	Sweet corn
	Sweet peas (frozen)
Hot peppers	
Kale/Collard greens	

Conversion Tables

Volume Equivalents (Liquid)

US STANDARD	US STANDARD (OUNCES)	METRIC (APPROXIMATE)
2 tablespoons	1 fl. oz.	30 mL
¼ cup	2 fl. oz.	60 mL
½ cup	4 fl. oz.	120 mL
1 cup	8 fl. oz.	240 mL
1½ cups	12 fl. oz.	355 mL
2 cups or 1 pint	16 fl. oz.	475 mL
4 cups or 1 quart	32 fl. oz.	1 L
1 gallon	128 fl. oz.	4 L

Oven Temperatures

FAHRENHEIT (F)	CELSIUS (C) (APPROXIMATE)
250	120
300	150
325	165
350	180
375	190
400	200
425	220
450	230

Volume Equivalents (Dry)

US STANDARD	METRIC (APPROXIMATE)
⅛ teaspoon	0.5 mL
¼ teaspoon	1 mL
½ teaspoon	2 mL
¾ teaspoon	4 mL
1 teaspoon	5 mL
1 tablespoon	15 mL
¼ cup	59 mL
⅓ cup	79 mL
½ cup	118 mL
⅔ cup	156 mL
¾ cup	177 mL
1 cup	235 mL
2 cups or 1 pint	475 mL
3 cups	700 mL
4 cups or 1 quart	1 L
½ gallon	2 L
1 gallon	4 L

Weight Equivalents

US STANDARD	METRIC (APPROXIMATE)
½ ounce	15 g
1 ounce	30 g
2 ounces	60 g
4 ounces	115 g
8 ounces	225 g
12 ounces	340 g
16 ounces or 1 pound	455 g

Resources

Most manuals for air fryers can be downloaded from the Internet. It can be helpful to download manuals for air fryers different from the one you own, to get more ideas and tips.

- **Manual for Philips HD9220/20** is found at http://www.p4c.philips.com/cgi-bin/cpindex.pl?ctn=HD9220/20&scy=GB&slg=ENG, and includes a user manual, quick start guide, and recipe booklet.

- **The GLiP Oil-less Air Fryer Instruction Manual** at http://www.homedepot.com/catalog/pdfImages/1f/1f683ead-1ebd-414d-add0-2d5a6ce0922e.pdf includes a helpful chart for cooking meats, potatoes, and snacks.

- **The Bellini Digital Air Fryer manual** is found at http://www.belliniappliances.com/electrical/documents/BTDF950_U&C_140730a.pdf and includes tips on maintenance and troubleshooting, as well as a cooking chart.

- **The GoWISE USA Air Fryer Instruction manual** is found at http://airfryerchips.com/wp-content/uploads/2015/10/GW22621_AirFryer_Manual.pdf and contains instructions for cleaning, troubleshooting, and a cooking guide.

- **The Todd English Air Fryer Manual** is found at http://www.manualslib.com/manual/975498/Todd-English-Teaf919.html?page=8#manual and includes quite a few easy recipes.

Some websites have delicious and easy recipes for the air fryer.

- **HotAirFrying.com** is maintained by Philips Air Fryers. This site includes ideas for using the air fryer in new ways, along with recipes for foods such as Crispy Jalapeño Poppers, Air Fried Tomatoes, and Green Curry Noodles.

- **Australian Allrecipes.com** (http://allrecipes.com.au) has a number of their top-rated, viewer-reviewed air fryer recipes, including Crumbed Chicken Tenderloins, Chocolate Cake in an Air Fryer, and Schnitzel Parmigiana.

- **YouTube.com** has quite a few videos showing exactly how to make many different recipes in the air fryer. Some of the recipes online include Spicy Roast Chicken, Bread Pakora, and Chicken Tandoori.

- **TheDallasSocials.com** is a blog all about the air fryer, with more than 100 recipes, such as Roasted Mushrooms, Mashed Potato Tater Tots, Fried Calamari, and Spicy Tuna Roll.

- **Airfry.blogspot.com** has some interesting and unusual vegetarian Indian recipes for the air fryer. They include Veggie Fingers, Falafel, and Cheese Spinach Balls.

Recipe Index

Index